The Small Living Guide for Compact Houses

Practical Strategies for Decluttering and Downsizing to Better Your Home and Life in 1000 Square Feet or Less

(Minimalism for Micro Living)

Written by:

Annette Maria Williams

Annette Maria Williams

www.MediaHomeHarmony.com

The Small Living Guide for Compact Houses

Dedication

I am so thankful for my Lord and Savior Jesus Christ and to my loving and supportive family!

<u>S</u>pecial Bonus!

Want this Book for FREE?

Get FREE unlimited access to it and all my new Books by joining the Fan Base!

Table of Contents

Introduction

The real estate market is changing every few years. When traditional homes are flying off the market and inventory is low, it is very hard for anyone to find the home of their dreams. Even when they enter the market, many homeowners find that anything of interest is selling for thousands above the asking price.

Not only are housing prices expensive but maintaining a big home can take a lot of time. More things can break, the landscaping takes forever, and the utility bills are slowly eating away at most of your income. This is not a good way to live your life. If you are sick and tired of wasting your time and money on a big home, you may wonder if there is a better way.

Small home living may be the solution. Get rid of the clutter, get rid of the wasted money, and the time it takes to maintain your dwelling while still having a nice place to call home. A small home may be smaller than you are used to, but with all the benefits, you will be able to make it work and enjoy life again.

I remember the time before we decided to move into a small home. We had reached the American dream. We built a large home, paid the mortgage, and worried about what would happen if something broke down, we went through a job loss or needed to do a lot of landscaping, fence repair, etc. It left us feeling depleted of time and in constant concern.

With a small home, things changed. We took a hard look at what we valued in life and decided it was time to make a change. With a small home, we could take on a lower mortgage payment, which freed up more money each month for things we actually wanted to do. We were able to pick a larger plot of land to put the house on, too, giving us more space and freedom.

You can choose to live the simple life too. You have the power to take control and reach homeownership without giving up all your time and money in the process.

Does this sound like the dream life you have been waiting for? Then this guidebook has the tips and tricks you need to jump right in and get the best results. From learning how to love small home living to being prepared through decluttering, organizing, decorating, planning, and purchasing the home, you will be ready to embrace this lifestyle and make it your own.

Small home living is not something that works for everyone. It does require some sacrifices, and if you do not make the right selection of small home types, you will end up way over your head. With the help of this guidebook, you can start learning right away, and the next time you come face to face with the inability to maintain your big home, you'll know exactly what to do.

About the Author

My name is Annette Maria Williams, and I am passionate about helping others discover the best ways to organize and decorate their homes. Not only have I dedicated time and attention to helping others declutter and de-stress from everyday life, but I am also an avid lover of the tiny home movement. I have been studying the different methods of living comfortably in small houses for many years and am excited to share some of my experience and knowledge with those who are ready to take the plunge and give tiny home living a try.

Small home living is a great idea for any stage in life. Do you want to live Off the Grid? Are you single, or do you want to have a smaller climate footprint? Are you an empty nester and no longer need a large home? Are you retired and want to downsize? Are you open to the different ways you can live small? Do you want more outdoor space for your children and pets? Have you been dreaming of living in a small or tiny home but are not sure where to get started? My goal with this guidebook is to help you achieve maximum comfort in your dream small house, no matter the size. These same tips helped me put together my own small home while feeling happy and fulfilled in the new space we call home.

As someone who has enjoyed small living spaces and joined the tiny home movement, I feel uniquely qualified to share my experience to help those who wish to make this their lifestyle. Small home living is not always glamorous. The space can be small and cramped, and unique challenges will arise as you adjust and try to fit in all your stuff. I am here to guide you through the change from a big home to a small one by providing step-by-step instructions that will help you get through the process.

I am excited to go on this journey with you. Since I am also a Professional Organizer, I enjoy organizing and working with people to help them become more organized no matter what size space in which they are currently living. My experience in small home living has shown me the advantages and beauty of giving up the big in favor of the small, and I am ready to share with you the no-fail way to enjoy a small home.

Keep reading to learn more about how great small home living can be and the steps that will help you reach your goals. I hope you enjoy this book!

Chapter 1

Loving Your Small Home

While many people are clamoring to get into a traditional home, this may not be the right option for everyone. There is a better way. For many, building or owning a small home will give them a chance for homeownership in an affordable manner. But what is a small home, why is it so popular, and how does it compare to living in a big (or traditional) home?

Benefits of Small Houses

There are many different options out there when you want to choose a new home for your needs. Some families do not want to downsize to smaller homes because they like having all the extra space. But for many individuals and families who are sick of all the costs of these bigger homes and tired of wasting their time cleaning and maintaining a big home, the small home can be one of their best decisions.

There are a lot of benefits to choosing to live in a small home rather than a traditional one in the United States. Some of the top benefits of going with a small home include:

Saves You Money

A small home is going to cost you a lot less money. This frees up your finances to help you pay down debt, go on vacation, or do some of the other things you want to do. Not only is the mortgage payment less, but you will find that the electric bill alone will be about $200 a month less in a 900 square foot home compared to a 3000 square foot home. That is an extra $2,400 a year you can save just on your utilities.

Many homeowners will choose to go with a small home because it allows them to live below their means and become more financially free. When you live below your means, you will be protected, even if you do end up with a financial setback at some point, rather than trying to handle a large mortgage.

Mortgage companies often allow borrowers to use up to 28% of their net income on the monthly mortgage payment, almost 1/3 of their income. The mortgage lenders may see this as affordable, but wouldn't you do better with your finances if you spent only 15% or less of your net income on housing? A smaller home makes this possible.

Easier to Clean

If you could choose between cleaning a 3000-square-foot home or a 1,000-square-foot home, which would you prefer? The 1,000 square foot home will take a lot less time than the other, and you will be able to make the home look as good as new in no time. Cleaning a large home (especially a two-story with a basement) can take up valuable time that you could be spending on other things, like having fun.

Small homes tend to get cluttered faster because of the limited space, but if you get in the habit of putting things away as soon as you are finished with them, it will make clean-up time go quicker.

Builds Up Your Relationships

Family bonding is encouraged: A smaller home allows you to have more social interaction between everyone in the family. There are fewer places for everyone to run off to and hide, and the tight spaces give it more of a comfy feel that is perfect for keeping the family close together.

The more space, the less time the family spends together. Dad could be downstairs playing video games, Mom may be in the laundry room folding clothes, and the kids are all in their own rooms. When the space is smaller, everyone will do the same activities, but they will be closer together and can spend that time bonding and enjoying each other's company.

Encourages Simple Living

Many homeowners love their small homes because they will have less space, which forces them to choose wisely what items deserve a spot in that space. A large home makes it easy just to purchase things to fill up that space. But you do not need all those items, and it just adds to the mess and the work you need to do in the home. Did you know that we only wear about 20% of our clothes 80% of the time? We can live with much smaller closets than we think we can.

A smaller home is mentally freeing: This follows the idea that the more we own, the more those items own us. Owning a larger home, with all the costs and extra items inside, can hold our mental energy hostage. The smaller home will have fewer responsibilities. It can be enjoyable to live simply and get out of debt.

Smaller environmental impact: To build a smaller home, you will use fewer resources. This can benefit the environment overall.

Easier to Customize the Home

If you live in a large home with big ceilings, two living rooms, and four bedrooms, it could be really expensive to furnish. This is even worse when it is time to decorate or remodel the home. Unless you are a high earner, it can be harder to make a large home inviting and warm.

Easier to Sell

If you ever do decide to sell the home, a smaller home will have a broader market. These homes are often more affordable than some of the other options, making them perfect for someone else someday who may need to stick within a budget when house shopping.

These are just some of the benefits of going with a small home rather than a big one. They may not be at the top of the list for some potential home buyers, but if you want to downsize your items and space, find an affordable home, and have a unique place to call home, then a small place is a perfect choice for you. The less you own, the less you have to maintain, store, insure, etc.

Small Houses vs. Big Houses

A small house provides an affordable housing option that makes you more financially stable and frees up so much of your time as well. But not everyone will benefit from choosing a small home, and some will still go for a big house.

For example, if you plan to live there with ten kids or have several generations living with one another, the big home will often work better and can fit everything you need at an affordable price. If you need to conduct business out of the home, a larger home will make the most sense too.

For many families, though, a big home is just too big. It makes it hard to be financially stable, encourages them to keep up with the Joneses in other parts of their lives, and just takes up a lot of their time.

Some of the advantages of choosing a big house instead of a small home include:

- Give each child their own bedroom for more privacy or to prevent fighting

- Have room for a dedicated office for you to run your business

- A larger kitchen for hosting gatherings

- Room to have some of your own individual interests, crafts, hobbies, exercise space

- More storage spaces

You may have imagined living in a mansion for years, but when it comes down to it, you must consider whether you would actually use all that space and if the cost would be worth it to you. Even though some of the benefits above can be nice, many individuals and families just do not feel the need to move into a large home.

Why Invest in a Small House?

While there are many benefits to moving into a smaller home, these places will have three main advantages over a big home. These include:

- Lower cost to purchase and maintain

- Less wasted space in the home

- Lower cooling and heating costs

For those who choose to invest in a small home, there are countless reasons why this may make a smart investment for them. A small home can mean quality splurges. You can make those luxury splurges you have always wanted. If you want granite countertops, they are much more affordable in a tiny home kitchen compared to a large home.

If you no longer want to rent and dream of having your own home on a limited budget, a small home can be a good investment.

Chapter 2

History of Small Living

This book covers small homes, and that includes tiny ones. The current definition of a Tiny House is - *A dwelling that is 400 sq. ft. (37 sq. m) or less in floor area, including lofts.*

Tiny homes have arguably been around for centuries. The log cabins found on the prairies were not big mansions, and only those with a lot of money, or the kings and queens of old, would have the types of large homes that we have in our modern times. In fact, a small home would have been large up until the last 100 years or so. It wasn't until much later that the idea of why a small or tiny home would become a virtue mainly because the homes had become so big.

One of the first writings about a tiny home was done by Henry David Thoreau in his story Walden. The book was written in 1854 and reflected simple living in natural surroundings. The story talked about how he lived in a 150- square-foot cabin near Walden Pond, and this type of living became the blueprint for many of the tiny house enthusiasts who picked it up over 150 years later. While small homes are bigger than this now, it is still a great story of how well we can live in far less space.

As we look through history, we can find that tiny and small homes were the norm for many individuals and families. The pioneers built smaller homes mostly meant just to sleep and eat in, while they spent the rest of the day doing work around the farm. The native tribes lived in teepees that were not very big either, with room to stay warm and snuggled together.

In the 1860s, the Republic of Texas issued land grants to settlers. It was part of the Peters Colony and one of the earliest settlements in Denton County, TX. The stipulation for someone to get the land was to build a cabin that measured at least 16 feet by 16 feet. If you are ever in Flower Mound, TX, you can see the log home settled by William Gibson of Missouri in its original spot. It was added onto over the years, but they have taken most of it down to what was built in the 1800s. Gibson was the first resident of the small cabin. He took an ax and cut down trees by hand, turning them into logs for the structure. They counted the rings on the logs to determine the tree's ages, and the home is now on the historical records. He also built the fireplace out of local stone, and it is still standing strong today!

For more information, go to - **https://www.flower-mound.com/2121/Gibson-Grant-Historic-Log-House**

So, how did the homes start to get so big? After World War II, many of the homes placed in the suburbs were averaging 850 square feet. This was a normal size home during that time, though it seems much smaller than we see today. It was throughout the course of the 20th century that the homes began to get bigger due to changes in government policy, a change in the American population seeing their houses not just as homes but as a financial asset, and the fact that the materials used to build the homes became less expensive.

When your home is an asset, and the costs of building a big home are not that expensive compared to the smaller homes, it is no wonder that many of the homes built throughout the 20th century were getting bigger and bigger. That is how we have gotten some of the large homes that we have today.

Real estate seems to go in cycles too. You can have a seller's market where the prices are high, interest rates are low, and there are few homes on the market. This causes bidding wars, and the sellers usually walk away as the winner. The next cycle that hits will be a buyer's market. This usually happens when interest rates start to go up, inflation goes up, and suddenly people can't afford their home utilities and maintenance and decide to sell. Most buyers can get a pretty good deal on a property, and if they have cash, it's even better.

While there have always been individuals who would like to go to a smaller home, it is believed that Jay Shafer was the one who jump-started the movement into tiny homes in 1999. Not all small homes are considered tiny homes, but the idea here is to appreciate the merits of simple living. In 1999, Jay Shafer not only published his first article about how great small living is, but he founded the Tumbleweed Tiny House Company, which was the first company to sell mobile tiny homes.

The tiny home movement was taking shape. It was sped along quite a bit in 2008 when the subprime mortgage crisis took hold in the United States, and foreclosure filings spiked more than 81%. With many people struggling to make their mortgage payments on those large homes and many people finding themselves in foreclosure, homebuyers wanted to ensure that this did not happen to them. Many people started to be interested in downsizing and living in more modest homes, including tiny homes and small homes.

While tiny homes often need special permits and can only be placed in certain spots because of their size and some of the adjustments needed due to their plumbing and electricity, things are a little different with a small home. The small home can be anything 1000 square feet or less, still allowing it to fit into what would be considered a "normal" size, although it is smaller than the average of 1600+ square feet.

You have probably seen tiny homes in your neighborhood, though most are older and come from the 1930s or before. If they come onto the market, they can naturally be less expensive because they have fewer square feet. Since these rarely come onto the market, though, often because not many are left, it is also possible to work with a construction home builder to help you create the perfect small home for your needs. Some companies have started doing this as their specialty.

Small Home Statistics

Small home living is changing how we look at our homes, and many, especially young people, have discovered that smaller can be better. Younger people would rather travel and have more adventures in life and aren't ready to settle down to a large home and mortgage.

How Many People Have Moved into Tiny Homes?

Individual areas show us there has been a big increase in the number of tiny home sales. For example, in New York City, it is estimated that 2.1% of all sales in real estate between 2010 to 2018 were tiny homes. It is not as common in Midwest areas, though. For example, tiny homes in Chicago represented only one-tenth of 1% of all real estate sales.

Sales estimates for tiny homes show us that the number of sales ranges from 2000 to 5000 a year. In 2017, there was a 67% increase in tiny home sales compared to 2016.

Currently 40% of retired Baby Boomers or those that are 50 years or older are tiny homeowners.

Millennials have a lot of college debt so 63% of them are interested in purchasing a small home. These two groups are projected to have the largest impact on sales of tiny homes in the future.

How Long Do People Live in Small Homes?

The amount of time an individual stays in a small home will depend on their situation. If a newly married couple moves into a small home and then has children, they are more likely to move out because they realize the space is too small for everything the baby needs, and that some of their needs in a home have changed. However, if someone purchases a tiny home and stays single or makes this purchase in retirement, they are more likely to stay in the home long-term.

The Best Locations in the United States for Living Small?

In some areas, it can be harder to build a tiny home. There are local regulations that may not like the way tiny homes are constructed, making them very unfriendly for those who would like to live there.

However, some states seem to welcome tiny and small homes and have no problem with people moving in or building their own. The top three states with the most tiny homes include California, Florida, and Colorado. California currently has 15.5% of all the tiny homes in the country, making it a great place to go if you want to enjoy nice weather and affordable tiny home living.

While individual states may be difficult with tiny homes, some individual towns in those states allow tiny homes. For example, the states of Oregon and Texas have towns specifically open to tiny homes for those who would like to build. A few of the tiny home friendly towns include:

Brevard, NC - Nestled in the heart of the Blue Ridge Mountains

Green Bridge Farm in Guyton, GA – One of the most popular and ecologically-friendly tiny house communities in the country.

Spur, TX - Declaring itself "the nation's first tiny house-friendly town".

Fresno, CA - Located in California's Central Valley

Salida, CO – This is a mountain town.

For more details see https://www.moving.com/tips/5-tiny-house-friendly-cities-in-america/

What are Tiny Houses on Wheels?

While many will choose a small or tiny home that will be their permanent residence and will not move around that much, some may look for different options; ones that allow them to be more mobile.

You can find many tiny homes to purchase on trailers. The maximum allowable size for a tiny house on a trailer is 8.5' wide, 40' long, and 13.5' high. That gives you a home of 320 square feet. To tow the home on most roads, the home and the tow vehicle combined can't exceed 65 feet.

If your tiny home exceeds 8.5' wide, it falls under the regulations for an oversized vehicle. Anything over 12' wide is classified as a wide load. Since you want a tiny home on wheels for convenience, a home that big would not be practical on wheels because it would become too expensive to move around.

Average Cost to Build a Tiny House

Just how much can you expect to spend when you build a tiny house? Research suggests that tiny houses range anywhere from $10,000 to over $150,000, but on average, you can expect to spend around $90,000.

Tiny homes come in all shapes and sizes. The design and execution of tiny homes depend on their owners' needs. In many communities, sharing facilities like bathrooms and kitchens can really change the needs and dimensions of the home.

A portable tiny home does not have one spot all its own. Some people want to avoid paying the property taxes of living in one area and would rather live on the road, wake up with a new view, or go down south for the winter. A portable tiny home will allow them to do this while bringing their home with them.

Small Home Community Vs. Owning Your Land

Many small homes are built on their own land. They could be outside of a town if the owner wants some freedom or space, or they could be the only small home on the block. One option that is growing in popularity is the small home community.

Small home communities are located in states that are friendly to the tiny home movement. They may be an area of a town or an individual town with these homes. Areas that have major housing crises are more likely to have small home communities. California, Texas, and Colorado are three states known for these small home communities.

What are the benefits of choosing a small home community versus moving into a small home individually? These include:

· **Sustainability:** All the homes near you are small and part of a community. You may find they value sustainability more and have a community garden or use special resources that help conserve energy.

· **Amenities:** Developers of a small home community are more likely to add facilities to the property to make it attractive to homeowners. These facilities may not be available to those outside the community. These can include pools, community centers, exercise rooms, etc.

· **Security:** The community knows one another and will work to provide security and keep the area safe for all who live there.

· **Community activities:** You will get a chance to be part of a larger group. This gives you more community activities to join. Sometimes these will be free to the residents.

If you want to move to an area with like-minded neighbors, then a small home community may make the most sense.

Owning Your Land

Small homeowners may choose to purchase land to place their tiny home. This gives them more freedom to live where they want. Many small homeowners want to have the ease of taking care of a small home and the lower costs, but they still want a lot of land or privacy. There are benefits and negatives to owning the land for your home. These include:

Benefits

- You may have more space since you spent less money on the home

- You can place the home anywhere on the property

- You do not have a HOA (Homeowner Association) to set the rules

- If you have at least an acre of land, you can always rent your land out to others with a tiny home. That can give you a bit of income and good use of the land.

Negatives

- Many areas do not allow tiny homes to be built there, limiting your land choices. Be sure to check the zoning laws for the land you want to purchase

- Your property taxes will be higher the more land you own

- Finding land and maintaining it can be challenging

- You will need to do a lot more to prepare the land for a home, such as clearing trees and bushes, putting in a driveway, getting utilities installed, putting up fences, etc.

Renting Your Land

Finding land to purchase can be difficult. Another option is to look for people willing to rent part of their land. They may just want to make some money on their vacant land. Others may need some services that may go with owning the land. Look online for people who are looking for landscapers to maintain the land. Perhaps they want a garden assistant, horse tender, pet sitter, or even a nanny. If any of those interest you, check on Airbnb for rentals. Talk to people in the zoning department in the area where you want to live. With some research and networking with others with the same interest, you may be able to find a good deal on a place to put your tiny home.

Chapter 3

Different Options for Small Home Living

There are many ways that you can choose to live small. You can go with an RV and visit RV parks around the country. This is attractive if you like to travel. Some choose to live Off The Grid out in the country. Others may want to rehab a storage container, a school bus, or an old shed. Tiny apartment living is possible, too, if you aren't quite ready for homeownership.

RV Living

Choosing to live in a small home does not mean you have to stay in one spot. You can hop into the RV, travel, and bring your home with you. This can be an exciting option, allowing you to have an adventure every day. Some families have two spots they go back and forth between based on the time of year, and others will travel around the country. Some RVs now even come with porches or patio decks. There are several different classes of Recreational Vehicles (RVs).

-Class A Motorhomes - These are homes on wheels. These vehicles range from 21-45 feet in length and are built on a heavy-duty chassis designed for driving.

-Class B Motorhomes - This is known as a "Camper Van" since it is a vehicle which is built just like a van. Placed on a standard van chassis, these vehicles include a raised roof so that you can easily stand up inside. They are usually smaller and easier to drive.

-Class C Motorhomes - These are a mid-size "drivable," 20-35 feet long. They have an over-the-cab area that provides extra sleeping or storage.

The next are different types of RV Travel Trailers. These are towable RVs or also known as a conventional travel trailer. They come in sizes from 4 feet to 35 feet long. They are towable by your car or truck, and a simple hitch system safely connects the towing vehicle to the trailer. The larger the RV model, the larger the towing capacity of your vehicle will need to be. The advantage is you can unhook them from your vehicle when you arrive at your destination, giving you a means of transportation. Some of the different kinds include – Pop-Up Campers, Fifth-Wheel Travel Trailers, and Sport Utility RVs (in case you have a lot of toys to take with you like motorcycles, canoes, or four-wheelers).

Pros and Cons of Living in an RV

Pros:

- Freedom to change your location at any time

- Less expensive than a home mortgage and property taxes

- Allows you to travel and enjoy nature

- No problems with neighbors. If you park next to someone you don't like, just move.

- Usually, it's easy to sell an RV if it's not the life for you

- No yard work or landscaping needed

- Many RV Parks have amenities like pools, mini golf, are near lakes, etc.

Cons:

- You will need to pay for all the repairs on the RV and keep it road-ready

- It is hard to make friends or a support group when you move all the time

- Healthcare can take a back seat when you travel

- Parking and storage for an RV can be a challenge

- Very little privacy, and some RV parks may not be safe

Long-term RV parks are a good option if you choose an RV as your small living home. They provide various amenities to make living there easier, such as onsite laundry, free WiFi, cable TV, swimming pools to wear out the kids, clean showers, restrooms, and possibly convenience stores if you need to grab something quick. Check the RV park to see whether they offer the amenities you need. The average monthly parking at an RV park is $400 a month, though some are more expensive and some that cost less. A private RV park can be nice for providing privacy and being safer, but they will often charge more for the spot you hold year-round.

If you plan to move around every few days, you will need to expect to pay $30 to $50 a night for your parking spot.

America is very RV friendly. Most of our roads are well maintained, and we have scenic highways, reasonable gas prices, and many places you could potentially pull over and park overnight to sleep.

If while traveling you need a quick overnight, I mean ONLY one night, there are several FREE places.

The suggestions below are mentioned because there are many of these businesses in the US; they are usually easy to find, have some privacy, and are normally safe and quiet.

-Walmart Parking Lots- Some stores even have free WiFi

-Rest Stops – Most have bathrooms, and some have picnic tables and pet areas

-Cracker Barrel Docking – These are usually right off the interstates. Be sure to have breakfast at the restaurant so they will continue to offer free RV parking.

Here are a few more businesses known to be friendly to overnight RV parking but be sure to check the business in the town you are visiting to ensure they are still welcoming RVs. They include-

-Bass Pro Shops

-Cabela's

-Camping World

-Costco

For a week-long stay, a public RV Park is a great option, but some are not maintained as well as others. I suggest checking with the websites below to get ratings for RV and campgrounds in the places you are interested in.

https://www.campgroundviews.com?aff=smallliving

https://www.goodsam.com/campgrounds-rv-parks/top-rated/

Mobile Home Parks

There are some amazing mobile home parks around the country. If you are over 55, Florida has parks right on the canals. You can step out your backdoor onto your dock for beautiful water views. It takes just minutes to hop on your boat and go for a ride down the canals. The HOA fees can be around $120 a month, but the amenities at some of these parks include: Large Clubhouses, Boat Slips, Fitness Centers, Marinas, Pools, Recreation Facilities, Tennis Courts, Community Boat Ramps, and Gated Security.

There are also "family friendly" mobile home parks around the country that can include a playground, pool, and bike paths.

What is a Yurt?

A yurt is a round tent-like dwelling made of a wood frame (often bamboo) and covered with heavy-duty cloth. It is sometimes defined as a circular tent of felt or skins on a collapsible framework. This modern adaptation of traditional Asian nomadic housing is becoming popular as a portable and spacious living solution.

The biggest difference between a tiny home and a yurt is the round shape. Some have built a Yurt as a tiny home with concrete or wood flooring and insulation. These are built more like cabins that don't collapse. You can purchase a kit at https://tinyhousetalk.com/how-to-build-your-own-freedom-yurt-cabin.

Living Small on a Boat

This is my favorite way to live small if you are a water person. It is just so relaxing to be around water.

Some people love the water, and some do not! If you don't like maintaining a yard, living on the water may be for you! I think it is important that you can swim, and you are not afraid of water. You need to make sure that you don't suffer from motion sickness too. Even when a boat is in a slip at a marina, if the weather gets bad, the waves can get rough and can really rock a boat.

It is also important to live in regions of the country where the lakes and rivers do not freeze. You can live on the water in the cold north, and some do, but it is much easier to live year-round on a boat that can stay in the water full time without worrying about the surrounding ice!

Marinas vs. Mooring Balls

Living on a boat in a marina is different from living at anchor or on a mooring buoy. On a buoy or mooring ball, you won't have access to 24/7 electricity and water. You are living off-grid when on a hook on the buoy. This can make a big difference, for instance if you want to have a <u>hot</u> shower every day. That is simple on a dock at the marina, but difficult if not impossible on the mooring ball.

The other nice thing about renting a slip at a marina is being able to walk off the boat onto your dock. Going back and forth in a dinghy every day can be a nuisance, especially if transporting large items such as furniture and heavy gear. Even groceries can get tedious using a dinghy.

Marina Living

The best part of a liveaboard boat is the company you keep and the places you can go. If you live at a marina, many will let you rent a covered slip monthly for a fraction of what an apartment would cost, and most include water in your slip fees. You usually have to pay for electricity. If it is an Army Corps of Engineers Lake

(https://corpslakes.erdc.dren.mil/visitors/visitors.cfm), they may ask that you only live there so many weeks of the month or year.

If you decide you don't like your boat slip neighbors, most marina's will let you change slips if other slips your size are available. They are rented by the foot, so for example, a 40 ft slip at an Oklahoma marina averages around $10 to $20 a foot or $400 to $800 a month. You can always go up a slip size, but usually, you need to have a slip at least as long as your boat. Some slips also offer decking for patio furniture, a refrigerator, and storage. Decking is a great solution if you need more storage. You can usually add dock boxes or larger storage cabinets to put on the decking area.

Some docks offer more things than others, which will also affect the slip price. Is the slip covered? Are there locking bathrooms with showers on the dock available only to renters of the slips? Is the lake view important to you? Do they offer WiFi?

Boats come in many sizes and shapes. Most liveaboard boats are cruisers, yachts, and houseboats. You can usually purchase a nice size liveaboard boat (over 30 feet long) for under $100,000, so it can be an affordable option to live on the water. Some are large enough to have two bedrooms and two bathrooms, and some have enough space for dishwashers and/or stackable washers and dryers. A houseboat is more house than boat with lots of floor space and even storage under the floor. To see before and after photos of the houseboat we refurbished –

https://www.mediahomeharmony.com/blogs/houseboat-remodel

A cruiser is usually more of a boat than a house and is great for travel, but the living spaces can be a little cramped. To save space, some cruisers have what is called a "wet bath" bathroom. That means the entire bathroom functions as a shower stall too.

Boat Bathrooms - Taking the boat to a pump-out station to clean out your bathroom tank is usually free at most marinas. Many marinas have companies that will also come to the boat, pump it out, and clean and flush your tanks.

Another nice perk about most marinas is they have locking entrance gates. Since you could be surrounded by million-dollar boats, it makes for a nice, gated community. Most marinas have security guards at night, so they are usually a safe option.

Many marinas are close to restaurants and parks. Marinas usually charge monthly for electricity. Some marinas raise their monthly slip fees every year, so you must consider all this in your budget. Any marina you visit, check their website or Facebook pages and look at the reviews to get an idea of what is or is not allowed.

While some of the best tiny home communities are in Colorado, California, and Texas, finding a good marina might be easier in Florida. 5th Street Marina and Miamarina are two great options for making your home on the ocean in Miami, FL. With the warm weather, you can spend all year in the marina, or you can choose to turn this into your home during the winter months. Berger's Marina in Lake of the Ozarks in Missouri, Marina Del Rey in California, and Elliot Bay in Washington are good options too.

If you decide you want to live on the ocean, there are many YouTube videos online of couples and even families who have chosen to travel on their 55 ft. catamarans full-time. Before that kind of adventure, I advise getting some boating experience by starting on a lake and getting your captain's license before trying the deep blue sea!

Some people also like to do the Great Loop starting in Florida on the Intercoastal Waterway (ICW). Since coastal states have a hurricane season, many boat owners will choose to move their boats more inland during that time. The Great Loop is a system of waterways that encompasses the eastern portion of the United States and part of Canada and gives boaters lots of options to move their boat around the country.

Dockominium

Another choice for small living on the water is a Dockominium. This is an apartment or condo based on the water. The Dockominium trend began in the early 1980s along the coastlines of Florida, Georgia, and North Carolina as boat owners sought to spend more time on the water at a time when government agencies conspired to limit available waterside access. Sometimes these are part of the marina, or it can be a standalone unit. They are often small, but they provide an affordable option for a waterfront home. They may include amenities just like a condominium on land. You can't move them or take them for a spin around the bay, so be sure you like the view and location of the dockominium you choose.

Small Apartments

Living in a smaller apartment is not much different from some traditional ones. Being willing to cut down on some of the space allows you to have more room for the luxury amenities you would like, such as granite countertops, energy-efficient appliances, and more. These are often less expensive than traditional apartments, too, so you can live in style while getting a chance to have all the luxury.

While homeownership is great, some individuals work in the city and do not want to commute miles from their homes every day. Some do not want the worry of maintaining the yard and the home. And still others like having people nearby and the feel of being in an apartment. A small apartment allows this to happen affordably.

A small apartment may be a good way to try out tiny living before you commit to purchasing a tiny home. If you rent for a year and decide you like it, then make the investment and buy something small.

Let's say your situation is like one of my clients. She had a house on a lake in Oklahoma and another large home in Venice, FL, and she sold them both to live in a small two-bedroom apartment. The first thing to remember is that you have fewer rooms and walls. The first thing to do is to sell all the large kitchen appliances with the homes since you won't be needing them in an apartment, and they probably won't fit in a tiny home. Sell most of the furniture in the rooms you no longer have, such as a large entryway, office, formal living room, formal dining room, and media room. Also sell most of the décor and artwork because you no longer have the wall space to hang the art. If you had five bedrooms and now you only have two, sell all but two of the bedroom sets, which include bed, dressers, nightstands, and lamps. My client kept too much of her living room furniture and felt cramped in her apartment. She eventually realized she needed to let go of more furniture to be comfortable in her current space.

Micro Apartments

There are also Micro Studio apartments in large cities that could be an option if you want to live simple but close to your workplace. The typical Micro Apartment is 150 to 350 sq. ft. In Japan, they are referred to as one-room mansions, and in the United Kingdom, they are called Micro Flats.

The typical Micro tenant is a minimalist. They describe themselves as someone that wants to live and travel rather than have a large place to collect a bunch of useless things.

See **www.LivingBigInATinyHouse.com** for more ideas.

Still want a garden but don't have a yard? One option is hydroponics gardening (gardens that only need water, and there are many books on that subject). You can also plant many vegetables in potted plants and put them on a windowsill, patio, or small balcony.

Helpful Items for Every Home

No matter which type of small home you choose, this is a list of things that can be very important to have on hand-

- First Aid Kit

- LifeVac Airway Clearance - for choking emergencies

- Working Fire Extinguisher

- Flashlights

- A lightweight Hammock – Never know when you will have unexpected guests

- Instant Pot – These can be used in many ways, such as a steamer, slow cooker, rice cooker, warmer, sterilizer, etc.

- Folding Wagon – It takes up very little space and is always handy to haul items.

- Folding Bike – These take up much less space than a regular bike and are fun to ride.

- Dissolving Toilet Paper – Get the bulk deal to always have at least a two-week supply on hand in case of panic buying

- Portable Gas Grill – The tabletop ones are compact enough to put on a small deck or patio and are easy to transport.

Chapter 4

Let's Declutter and Organize

When you live in a tiny or small home, your space will be more limited. You need to be really careful about how you use your space. Clutter not only causes depression and anxiety, but it can make it more difficult to live in that tiny space. Learning how to declutter and organize your spaces will make a big difference in how much you can enjoy your home.

Signs That You Need to Declutter Your Home

Living in a small home can seem impossible when you first move in. It is a much smaller space than many are used to, and they may worry that they won't be able to make it happen. The problem may be more related to having too many material items rather than not having enough space.

Many homes need to consider going through a decluttering phase. This time allows them to take a hard look at all the items inside and decide what to keep and throw out. This can free up so much space and make the area more comfortable to live in, no matter how big or small.

There are a few signs you can look for to help you determine whether it is time to declutter your living space. These signs include:

- It is hard to find things: The first sign of clutter that most homeowners notice is that they can't find the items they need. When you clear out the clutter and organize your items in the home, you will find it easier to find the important items you need daily.

- You can't close the drawers: Your cabinets and drawers should close with ease. If you must force it, you have too many items in the drawer.

- You have piles of papers: Papers can add up. Between the bills, kids' paperwork, and stuff from work, the papers can be all over the place. It is much better to get an organization system in place and throw out anything you don't need. Purchasing a paper shredder can be useful. Most papers like personal taxes can be disposed of after seven years, so only keep the most current papers. Always trying to do more business on your computer and going paperless as much as possible will help keep the paper monster at bay. When I find something interesting on the internet and want to remember where it is, I create a file and copy and paste the link to the article in case I want to refer to it. If it is just a one-page article or I am concerned that it will not be posted online for a long time, I will sometimes just take a photo and then file it on my computer. Remember, you don't have to print the internet!

- There is no space on the counters: Your counters and other flat surfaces on tables, dressers, and hutches should be primarily clear most of the time. This can seem almost impossible with kids, but you should be able to clean them off weekly. If the items need to stay there because you have nowhere else to put them, it is time for you to do a good decluttering session.

- You can't fit the car in the garage: Your garage is meant to store your cars and a few other outside items you may need, such as gardening tools and things to fix the home. When the garage gets so packed that you can't fit the car in, it means you have too much stuff.

- You spend a lot of time cleaning: Papers should be organized in filing cabinets, books on shelves, toys should be in bins, clothes and shoes should be in closets, and food/kitchen items should be in cabinets or a pantry.

Recognizing the signs of clutter early on, especially in a small home, can help you keep it under control.

Benefits of Decluttering Immediately

Decluttering may seem like a waste of time. You must go through each room of your home to get rid of items, and you may not have the time or the patience to get it all done. This is a task that may seem better left to do down the road. But whether you live in a small home or a big home, decluttering can make your life easier, and it is so important.

You must think of yourself as a minimalist in training. It is really difficult to go from consumerism to minimalist in just a day or two. Give yourself some time to start thinking about living with less.

First, decluttering will be a great way to save money. When you systematically declutter the home, you come face to face with some of your past purchasing decisions. You realize how bad those decisions were and why it is so bad to hold onto the clutter around the home. It may be enough to help you become more careful about your shopping habits. Plus, you won't have to search around for items or double purchase because you can't find something.

Decluttering your home can also lead to less stress. Studies show us that clutter increases cortisol levels in women more dramatically than in men. But when the mom of the home is stressed out from the clutter, this is enough to carry over to other family members as well. Having more stuff than you can maintain can be stressful for parents and their kids. Taking a good hard look at what is in your home and scaling it down can help reduce these stress levels and free up your mind and energy for other things.

It also becomes easier to maintain your home when there is less clutter and fewer distractions. You are not constantly just putting the items away, waiting for them to fall out of the cabinet; you are removing them from your home completely. This helps keep the home organized and prevents issues with having to pick it up again in a few days. A small home without the clutter can be infinitely easier to maintain. Keep a nice basket by the front door or a box in the closet and every time you find something that you no longer need, put it in the container. Once the container is full, put it in your car and take it to a donation center. When you return with your empty container, put it back to continue the process of constantly purging items no longer needed.

Your sleep can be improved when you choose to declutter. When you have a ton of clutter around you, especially in the bedroom, it can interrupt your sleeping patterns because it will fill your mind with anxiety and thoughts of living in a mess. If you have trouble getting to sleep at night, you may need to clear out the room.

Whether you go all out and decide to do the whole house in a weekend or take it room by room, you will see a big difference in the quality of life and the amount of space you have when you decide to declutter.

Another option is to hire a Professional Organizer. They can do the job quicker and more efficiently. They can set up systems for you to be able to maintain a clutter-free home. They also know about some of the best organizing products to keep the space organized once they have helped you sort and purge the items you no longer need.

How to Identify and Let Go of Items that You Don't Need Anymore

The trick to decluttering is that you must get rid of the items that just take up space and serve no purpose to you any longer. This can start with all the trash that you haven't had time to pick up but also moves on to other items important at one time but just taking up space now.

For some, distinguishing between the items that need to go and the ones that can stay is the hardest part of the process. This part is imperative if you do not want all those items to hang around your home for years to come.

One way to think about it is to get rid of everything you don't want others to know you have before you die. That diary you had in junior high is really not worth keeping! I worked with a lady a few years ago who would buy things on the shopping networks when she got bored. She didn't just buy one item because if you only have room for one candle, they come in a case of three, and you must buy all three! She had filled up two storage units with all the blankets, beach towels, umbrellas, soaps, lotions, candles, Christmas decor, T-shirts, and other clothes. We encouraged her to start giving some of it away since it was all new and still in the boxes or bags. Getting rid of our abundance of things can make life more pleasant.

Another client that we helped had rented a storage unit for over ten years. When we helped her unpack it all, she discovered that most of it she didn't want or need anymore, and it was donated or trashed. We estimated that she had spent over $49,000 in the last ten years for things she no longer needed! Rental storage units should always be temporary. If you have been renting one for more than a year, it is time to clean it out and remove the items. If you haven't missed the items in a year, you really don't need them.

If you no longer use the item, donate it to someone who can use it. I always recommend donating an item before putting it in the trash because our landfills are filling up way too fast. Even though we can't use the pet items anymore, if they are still in good shape, someone else may be getting that first pet and need those items.

Ask yourself, if you were to lose everything in your home, what is the bare minimum you would need to purchase again? Most of us don't need four sets of linens when two for each size bed in the home will work just fine. One blanket for each bed is also more than enough.

There are a few things that you can do to make decluttering easier, especially if you are someone who struggles to let go of items. Some of these steps include:

- Give yourself a challenge: Turn the process of decluttering into a challenge or make it into a game. See if you can get rid of thirty items in each room or if you can make your pile of keep items smaller than the pile of purge items. You can choose the decluttering process but find a way to turn it into something fun.

- While purging, if you think you are going to need something again someday, just remember, if the cost of the item is less than $20, you can just go buy it <u>when and if</u> you ever need it again.

- Try to remember the last time you used the item: This works really well for clothes. If you can't remember the last time you wore the outfit, it is time to donate. An excellent time to do this is when the weather season changes. If you didn't wear the sweater at all last winter, you probably won't wear it next winter either. When you get out the summer clothes, if it doesn't fit, donate it. It also may be time to donate those short shorts.

- If you haven't looked at the memento for years and can't remember where it came from, take a photo of the keepsake and donate it.

- Get rid of papers: You do not need to keep all the papers your children bring home from school. Store the items that you absolutely need, and then dump the rest. The easiest way to do that is to keep only the things you think the children will want to see again in 20 years. They probably won't care about that 1st place ribbon if every kid in class got the same ribbon. They won't care about the math test, but if they write a story and get an A on the paper, that may be something they would want to see again. Since children bring home papers all year long, it is best just to keep a bin for each child and then at the end of the school year, go through the bin of papers and only keep the best. That way, you don't have to go through the papers constantly because if you wait till the end of the year, you will find lots of duplicates that can be thrown away.

- Get rid of doubles: As you sort through your home, get rid of anything doubled up. You do not have room for five of the same kind of pots in your small kitchen, and it is unlikely that you are using all of them. You do not need 20 beach towels when only two people live in the home. Great space savers for towels are the ultra-soft microfiber camping towels. They dry quickly, are lightweight, and are easy to store.

- Consider What do I Want to Keep? The biggest issue in decluttering is too much focus on what you need to get rid of in your home. To turn this around, think about all the things you would like to keep. This makes the process more positive and allows you to pick items that you truly love and use, rather than being sad that you are getting rid of too much.

Decluttering and Organizing Room By Room Guide

Each room in your home will need some special attention to help you reach your goals and clear up some of the space that you need. Always divide your belongings into categories to help you sort more efficiently.

For each room, have 4 containers labeled -

- Keep

- Donate or Sell

- Trash

- Belongs in another room

Living Room

In a smaller living room, even a little bit of clutter will make the room look messy. This is a great room to start your decluttering process.

Start with a quick sweep of all the items hanging out in the living room that do not belong there. You should not have papers on the table; the movies and the books should be on a shelf. All flat surfaces should be clean when you are done. Put your trash in the bag and donate old electronics you are holding on to. Take your old computers to a computer store like Best Buy, and they can help you wipe out the hard drive of any personal information. There are usually electronic recycle places in large cities that will take your broken flat screen TVs, etc.

Start with One Desk Drawer

If you have a desk or other drawers in the living room, such as an end table drawer, then it is time to clean them out. Don't feel overwhelmed here. Start with just one. The papers you need to keep should go in a box labeled – to be filed. Put the old knick-knacks in your donation box and free up that prime real estate space for something you use often.

Give the Bookshelf a Makeover

Organize the games and books you would like to keep, discarding ones that are in bad shape or never used. Then look at the other items on the shelf and decide whether you would like to keep them or if they take up too much space. If you plan to keep an item, then it needs to get a "home" to keep it organized. If you have shelves of DVDs or CDs, it is time to donate and go digital because you no longer have the space to store those items.

Curb the Collectibles

Collections can easily take over your storage space in a small home and make it look cluttered. These may be treasured keepsakes, but unless you have a place to display and enjoy them, it may be time to give them to your children or grandchildren. With limited space comes limited storage.

Large collections of collectibles will display the best in these situations when you can show them off in bits and pieces rather than all simultaneously. Think about what you would like to see all the time around the home, things that hold the best memories, and utilize those in your decorating.

Creating a Play Zone

Your kids likely have games, books, papers, backpacks, and clothes all over the floor. You can have them keep these items in their room. Or, if you like to keep these centrally located, choose to get bins to keep all those extras in one place.

Since we all know that stuffed animals multiply in the night when we are asleep, a good way to store all those creatures is to get a bean bag chair or ottoman without the beans! Just fill it up with the stuffed animals, so it becomes a chair and storage space simultaneously.

You can even hang up some of the artwork you would like to keep in one area; just be prepared to switch it out every few months. They make wall frames with doors that can hold a stack of kid's artwork and can easily be changed to display different art. Another fun idea is to put up a Lego wall for kids to play on without taking up a lot of floor space.

Unused corners of the living room can turn into a fantastic play area because the walls can help block the clutter. A child's size folding table and chairs can be helpful since it can be folded out of the way when not in use. A bookcase and stackable drawers or bins can help store toys. The wall cube systems are great for kids. You can add doors, drawers, and various cube inserts to contain small items.

Each cube should be labeled so that toys find their way back to their proper home. The cube inserts can also be used to set thresholds for toy accumulation and clutter. For example, if the cube for balls is full, then no more balls can be added unless some are eliminated (donated) so that all balls fit into one cube. Then consider a rule that only two cubes of toys can be out at one time.

Pet Areas

We all love our pets, but they do come with lots of extra items. A large dog can take up a lot of space when it comes to a place to sleep, storing their food, and keeping a place for their chew bones and toys. Maybe consider an outside pet with its own tiny home like a doghouse.

If you are gone all day for work, it might be better to get an independent cat that won't care that you are not home. You will, of course, need a place to keep their food, litter, and toys too.

A handy place to put dog or cat food and water bowls is the kick plate under your kitchen counters close to the sink. These can be pulled out while the animal is eating and then slide the drawer back under the cabinet when done.

Most cats and dogs need sunlight and a place to roam daily. For cats, you can put some carpet-covered floating shelves in front of your windows to give them a place to climb and look outside.

Kitchen

Your kitchen can present some unique challenges in a small home. You still want to bake and cook like before, but some kitchen appliances can take up a lot of room and are harder to fit into the small space. There are a few steps that the homeowner can take to help declutter their kitchen including:

- Evaluate your utensils: Decide which utensils you would like to keep in the kitchen. Before keeping an item, decide whether other similar kitchen items can do the same task. For example, an apple slicer is nice, but a knife can do the same job.

- Put the important stuff upfront: Stop wasting a lot of time looking for all the items you need each day and use some magnetic caddies to help keep those items right where you need them. A magnetic strip on the wall can hold knives. Magnetic tins that attach to your fridge can hold spices. The best place to put your most used items is to put them in cabinets and drawers between knee and shoulder height. This is called the "prime real-estate" storage area. Store items you don't use as much on the top or bottom of cabinets.

- Streamline the plastic grocery bags: Plastic bags can be nice for holding items and lining small trash cans, but they will quickly make a mess if you are not careful. Choose a dispenser that can be hung on the wall in a cabinet or pantry to hold the bags in one small area until you need them.

- Use a rolling cart: In a small home, your options for storage in the kitchen will be limited. But a rolling cart can help. This can help you utilize that small amount of space between the counters and the fridge or table to hold some of the items you need.

- Check expiration dates on all canned goods, spices, and items in the fridge. Discard all that have expired.

- Install some cabinet racks: A simple storage rack inside your cabinets can allow you to have twice as many things inside that space. If you have wall space, pick decorative racks that will hold extra kitchen items.

- Purge your utensil drawer: Your utensil drawer can quickly become overrun if you are not careful. Look into an organizer that will help you put the silverware and other items in an easy-to-access area. The other day we bought some new knives. Even though I am a Professional Organizer, I don't always take the time to follow my own advice. I noticed that four of my kitchen drawers were unorganized, and there were things in the drawers that we no longer used. Since we needed a spot for the new knives, it was time to get rid of many of the old, dull knives filling up the space. We took the time to test each butcher knife, carving knife, steak knife, etc. We ended up donating about 20 knives that we had duplicates or were not worth taking the time to sharpen. Once that was done, I put all the "like" things together, and it gave us a lot more room in the drawers. It makes cooking a lot easier to find the utensils we need quickly.

- A cabinet for the kids: Your kids often have many items that need to fit into your small kitchen space. Why not give them a drawer or a couple of containers in a cabinet for all their cups, plates, etc. This can help you find everything you need for them, including their lunchbox and other lunch supplies to make each morning a little more efficient.

- When choosing storage containers, always go with clear ones! This will make it easier for you to tell immediately what you have available and what is running low. Use labels on containers so everyone learns where things belong and can return items quickly. Cabinet and drawer organizers are your friends!

- Use a dry-erase board: Add this to your pantry door to help you track your grocery needs and what chores and notes you need to remember. Make sure to hang it in a place you can see and keep a few markers on hand. When you are ready to go grocery shopping, take a photo of the whiteboard grocery list with your cell phone, so you have the list when you arrive at the store.

- Stow your small appliances: It is easy to leave the appliances on the counter, but they take up some of the valuable kitchen counter space. I have a fold-up air fryer that takes up very little space on my countertop. When we need to use it, it just flips down and is ready to go. You can do many things with this one appliance- Air Fry, Air Roast, Air Broil, Bake, Toast, Dehydrate, and it is a Warmer too … see my Free Book for more info. If you have a pantry, this is the best place for small appliances. If not, storing them in a lower cabinet works if you do not use them frequently. Utilize a retractable pantry drawer for small appliances that you use often. You just pull it out when using, and then push it back when finished. If you still have the bread maker, it takes up a lot of space, and if you are not using it weekly, it may be time to donate.

- Downsize the tableware: Think about the exact number of plates, bowls, utensils, and glasses that you actually use each day, and get rid of the rest. This can help keep the kitchen clean because you will need to wash the dishes right away.

- Some people love their set of Christmas dishes. Even though they can be beautiful, they can take up a ton of cabinet space. Since you only use these once a year, I highly recommend donating or selling the holiday sets, only keeping what you use daily. A holiday party can be a lot easier with disposable plates and utensils. It makes clean-up quick, and as long as you have a trash can within easy reach, your guest will usually help.

- Limit the pots and pans: You can probably make most of your meals with fewer pots and pans. You can consider getting medium-sized pots to help handle most of the cooking you need to get done each day. They make some amazing skillets that will go from stovetop to the oven, and they are also dishwasher safe. This can give you a skillet and baking dish all in one! They can save you both space and time in the kitchen because you won't have as many pans to store and wash. Since your pots and pans can take up a lot of room in the kitchen, consider getting a hanging pot rack to put them up and out of the way.

- If you have an open kitchen concept home, an island on wheels can give you more options. It provides more counter space to prep meals, more storage space, and can also be used as an eating area. If you have company over, you can move the island against the wall, use it as a buffet, and have additional space for guests to mingle.

- Limit the bulky items: A big cookie jar can be decorative and fun, but it will eat your counter space. Keep only the items you can use without taking up valuable real estate in the kitchen. Many collapsible kitchen items can really help with limited storage. A few are: collapsible dish drying rack, collapsible strainers and colanders, collapsible measuring cups and spoons, collapsible funnels, and food storage containers.

- Mesh bags hung on the wall on hooks in a tiny kitchen can hold bulky items like fruits and vegetables. Hanging the produce can help it last longer too! If you have a pantry, consider hanging aprons and potholders on hooks on the pantry door or wall.

- One trick to remember is to know your own culinary strengths. Keep the kitchen items that help you cook the items you like now, not the foods that you dream of cooking in the future. If you are not big into baking, you probably do not need cupcake tins in the cupboard, and if you never make a cheese plate, that cheese board is just going to collect dust. Only keep the items you plan to use.

Dining Spaces

Your dining room is going to be a great place for the whole family to spend time.

- Get in the habit of cleaning up the table after every meal

- Again, sort items and make a pile of everything that needs to go into another room.

- With what is left, it is time to sort and throw away anything old and no longer needed.

- Once the table, any sideboard shelves, and other surfaces in the dining room are in order, it is time to get the table decorated. Adding a centerpiece to the table will help keep it dressed, and hopefully, it won't become a catch-all for everything that comes in the front door.

- If you want to keep extra things in the dining area, consider how you would organize it. Many families like to have Bible studies around the dinner table, or this is where the children do their homework. Having a place for study materials on a bookshelf or a sideboard can be helpful.

I just helped a client with three sons in elementary school. After doing homework, they would leave papers, pencils, crayons, etc., on the dining table. She purchased three 15 x 13 decorative baskets, one for each child. We put their names on their baskets and created a system for them. When they finished their homework, they had to put all their supplies back in their basket. The homework and books that needed to go back to school were all put in their backpacks. The backpacks then needed to be put on a hook by the door so they were easy to grab for school the next day. Before sitting down for dinner, they had to take their basket to their room. Since boys always seem to be hungry, it helped them get their homework done efficiently and things picked up quicker. It would stay in their rooms on the weekends, and then the basket could come out again on Mondays when they had homework. It really helped keep the dining space tidy.

Bedrooms

Your bedroom should be an oasis, an area that helps you get to sleep at night and feel well-rested when you get up. When there is a lot of clutter in the way, this becomes really hard to do. Everything in your bedroom should be there for relaxation and comfort to help aid you in this goal.

Start with the bed. Think about fabrics, pillows, and other items that will help you feel comfortable and ready to jump in and fall asleep. Some like to have a ton of pillows and blankets around; you no longer have the room for that, so just keep it simple. Take the time to make the bed each morning to keep the room neat and tidy.

Next, take all the papers out. Bills and other papers may be important, but they will interfere with your ability to calm down and sleep. And they leave a lot of clutter. All your papers should be in one area of the home. The best place is an office, but if you don't have the space for that, then in the dining area where you have a surface to pay the bills and a small place to file papers that you need to keep. Keep them as far from your bedroom as possible, so they do not cause you a lot of anxiety.

If you are like many homeowners, you will have a lot of technology in your bedroom. This can be work equipment, like your computer, or something for play, like your television. This is a bad idea. Technology can disrupt your sleep and clutter up the room. Even your phone should be placed on a curfew an hour before sleep to keep you from wasting time before bed. Spend that time reading and socializing with your loved one rather than letting the technology take over.

A quick decluttering sweep in your bedroom can make a big difference. The steps are simple here but make sure you have your four containers labeled -Keep, Donate or Sell, Trash, Belongs in another room.

- Use the space under the bed: Your bed is slightly raised off the floor. This is a great space that can help store some of the items you need without them being in the way. Think about putting some of the extra blankets that you need only in the winter, or even storing clothes out of season. This is also a good place for keepsakes or items you don't need often.

- When your bedroom is small, or your children's bedroom is small, think about putting your artwork/photos on the walls. This is preferable to putting it on your nightstand or the dresser, which may have limited surface space.

- Declutter your closet: it is easy to throw anything and everything into the closet to get it out of sight. Take all the items out of the closet and sort everything into several piles. Every item needs to go into one of the labeled containers as mentioned above. If you have not seen the item for six months and it has been longer since you wore it, do not add to the "keep" pile unless it is very valuable, like your wedding dress. Be selective here. Put likes together, for example, all your dresses together by length and color, jeans together, all your T-shirts together by color. You may decide you don't really need five red skirts, and you can donate four of them for someone else to enjoy. When you are finished, put the "keep" pile back into the closet by item and then color.

- Plastic vacuum bags are great for linens and help keep a lot in a limited space on a shelf.

- Use a laundry basket to keep the clothes off the floor and a cute trash can so you are not tempted to leave bottles, tissues, and other trash all over the place. They make collapsible laundry baskets that can be hung on the wall when not in use.

- Get a functional nightstand: A decorated nightstand can be nice, but it may take up more space than you have. A small nightstand with a drawer works well for storing a few items without being too big in the space.

- With limited floor space, consider a tall chest of drawers to help with clothes storage.

- If you have at least three inches of space behind the door between the door and the wall, you can also purchase a Cabidor. They go on existing door hinges, perfect for apartments because you can easily take them down when moving. They have several shelves and hold small items like makeup or medicines. I put wrapping paper rolls in the one I have.

- If you think you still need an iron and ironing board (Permanent Press … Hello!), then get a fold-down one that fits between the studs. There is enough shelf room for spray starch bottles and the iron, and it only sticks out of the wall about three inches. These fit great behind a laundry room door.

Bathrooms

The bathroom tends to collect many items, especially if you are in a home with one or two bathrooms for the whole family to share, rather than three or four like the bigger homes. Some things that help organize your bathroom include:

- Sort through all the items and put all the "like" items together to see what you have for duplicates. Get rid of anything that is old or no longer serves a purpose.

- Makeup has expiration dates, so check those and discard if it has expired. Old makeup can be a breeding ground for germs. Toss mascara after three months, liquid foundation after six months and lipstick after two years.

- Be sure and discard all expired medications properly.

- After purging, the next goal is to make sure as few items as possible are on the counters. It is easy to set things down on the counters and forget they are there, but everything in the bathroom needs to have its own place. As you clean the bathroom, make sure one of the storage areas is not the counter unless you have a nice container to keep the items together.

- Use the doors: Many people know they can place items inside the cabinets, but they do not think about using the inside of the cabinet door to hold some of the items as well. Consider getting hooks or working with little storage bins to hold some of the items that you need. A shoe holder with clear pockets is great for holding small bathroom items behind the main bathroom door. You can also get shower curtains with pockets to hold the items you need when bathing.

- Bring in the drawer dividers: Rather than letting the items in the drawers go all over the place, get some drawer dividers to keep things more organized and easier to find.

- Each family member should have their own caddy to hold the items they need. They can just pull out the caddy, use their items without searching, and then put it all back when they are done.

- Keep a laundry bin in the bathroom: This is the perfect place for all those dirty towels and other clothing items to go when your family is done with them.

- Use a hook instead of a bar: A towel bar takes up more space than a hook, and your towels may dry faster when you hang them on a hook.

- The outlet shelf is really handy for an electric toothbrush, cell phone charger, etc., to free up counter space. There is a photo of these in my Free Book for more details.

- Something as simple as rolling towels up and putting them on a shelf can take up less space in a cabinet. Many small homes also consider getting rid of the bathtub because this takes up a lot of valuable space on the floor, and a shower can do the same thing. The shower is often a safer option when getting in and out.

- Unique shelving can be helpful in the bathroom. You need to keep your items organized and easy to reach. You could throw them in the vanity drawer, but this will become unmanageable quickly because you can't immediately see what is in the drawer. A better option is to choose a few unique shelves with cute containers that can work as some of the decorations. Again, have a container for each family member to store their toiletries. Labels are important to be sure everyone knows where their items belong. There are lots of cute decorative labels that you can purchase.

- They now have lighting built into the mirror. It can go all around the mirror or just on each side. This eliminates having to hang lights on the wall or from the ceiling and can give you more space for shelves or hooks.

- To save much-needed space and hide the mess, you can purchase a small trash can that also holds the toilet brush and extra can liners.

Garage and Storage Shed

With the inside of the home decluttered, it is time to move on to other parts. Your garage and/or storage shed is next on the list. You should have enough room in the garage to fit your car (or two cars if the garage is that big), but it is easy for clutter to build up over time in the garage. Many homeowners will just throw unwanted items or items without a specific space in the home into the garage, and soon they can't walk through their garage.

The garage can take a bit of time because not only do you need to get rid of items, but you must also devise a plan that will help you organize some of the big items you plan to keep. Some steps you can use to help clean out the garage include:

- Assess the mess: Move the car to the driveway and keep the garage door open, so you have space to sort everything in the garage. Set up a table so you can really see the items. You will quickly realize that you have duplicates of many items once you sort and go through the entire garage. Keep a few trash bags or boxes ready and follow the keep, donate, sell, recycle, or trash system to help you organize.

- Create dedicated zones: Once the items are sorted, and you have decided what you want to keep, then it is time to zone the different areas. All the gardening tools need to be organized next to each other, and then the camping gear can be in another area. Create a tool area where they can be accessed easily, like in a rolling tool cabinet with drawers to keep them organized. Sporting equipment can also be put in another area. Depending on how often they are used, some seasonal sporting items can be stored on overhead hanging racks placed over the car, so it doesn't take up floor space. That is also a good place to store holiday items since they are only needed once a year. Keep like items in clear plastic bins with locking lids. Do not use cardboard boxes because they tend to attract insects. Once you have contained the items, be sure to label the container with the content, so everyone in the family will know where the items are stored. This will help keep the garage organized while helping you find what you need the next time you search for it.

- Metal rolling shelves on wheels are handy for garages to store your plastic containers. When a shelf is on wheels, it is easy to move when cleaning or if you decide to move it across to the other wall of the garage

- Check the garage door opener: Take some time to check whether the doors still operate as they should. Do you feel a draft when the door is closed, or is it time to fix some of the weather stripping around the edges? Get this fixed now to help keep dust, bugs, and rodents out of your garage.

- Vertical space is often forgotten in garages. They have wall-hanging racks to store your mops, brooms, rakes, and other garden tools. This can help maintain the organization and keep items off the floor.

As you move into a small home, you will need to make the most of every space you have. With a little bit of creativity and downsizing, you will find that a small home has plenty of room for you and your family to love.

Decluttering Never Ends

Decluttering is not a one-time thing. It would be nice to throw out a ton and clean up one time, but we must be actively working to prevent the clutter from coming back.

You can do several things to declutter and maintain the space you need constantly. Some of these include:

· Commit to tossing, donating, or recycling any item that is not needed, wanted, or used. Before it comes into your home, decide what the item's purpose is and if you really need it.

· Focus on just one area at a time. Often it is best to start working on the area that is the most bothersome.

· Set a timer to help you concentrate on the work that needs to get done. The Pomodoro technique is great here. You set the time for 20 to 30 minutes and work non-stop, with no distractions. When that time is up, take a five-minute break. Repeat two more times. You can then take a longer break or call it good for the day. Repeat as often as you need.

· Declutter as a family. Decluttering a whole home on your own can take forever and may seem overwhelming. You need to work together to get it done faster. Start with a room that everyone uses and have each person take a section of the room.

· Sell the unwanted items. You can use the money for a fun night out or help with some other purchases you need to make.

· Be in control of the papers. Papers can quickly pile up in any home. Each day when you get the mail, immediately open, sort, and put the junk mail in the recyclable bin. Put bills that need to be filed in a "to be filed" box. Once a month, take the time to file papers you need to keep in your file cabinet. Put anything that needs to be scheduled on your calendar, for example, wedding and graduation invitations.

· Take 15 minutes a day to help pick up the home, and this will keep the clutter to a minimum.

Some families start a rule for every item they bring into the home; they make themselves get rid of one item, too, keeping the cycle of decluttering going.

Chapter 5

The hardest part about Downsizing

What to Do If You Feel Too Attached to an Item that You Can't Throw it Away? (AKA - Sentimental Items)

You are working hard to declutter your home, and then you run into an item that holds a lot of sentimental value to you. You may not use the item, may not need the item, and may not even like the item. But you have a sentimental attachment to it, making it hard to get rid of it. I get it!

When we moved into a smaller home, since I am a very sentimental person, getting rid of family items that I had for years was really hard! Since I was the youngest child of the youngest child of nine, all my grandparents died before I was born. Since I never knew them, some of their items are very precious to me, and so family heirlooms are things I always want to keep.

The thought of getting rid of an item can seem impossible, but even sentimental clutter can cause you harm in other ways. It can add a lot of stress to your life, and you may not have room for that item in your small home. So, how are you supposed to get rid of it?

Get Rid of the Guilt

The first step here is to let go of the guilt. Take a dive into your emotions. If the only reason you keep the item is from guilt, then it is time to let it go. If the emotion is love or nostalgia, that is a little better, and you can try out a few of the other tips to help.

Let in the Vulnerability

Once you determine the emotions around the item are nostalgia or love, then it is time to let in the vulnerability. You do not need to push aside the emotions. Let it in, and then make a purposeful choice about whether that item should stay. It does make the process take longer but allows you to keep some of the things that hold the most value to you.

Take Pictures

Creating a digital photo album takes up little space. Take a picture of the old awards and report cards and anything else you would like to remember, and then let the physical item go.

Ask Yourself the Right Questions

Many assume that asking themselves, "Does this item bring me joy?" will be enough to help them know whether to keep an item or not. But this doesn't really work for sentimental items. Your questions need to be more focused here including:

- What do I need to keep in this season of life?

- What items do you truly want to keep without feeling obligated to do it?

- Could someone else benefit more from the item than I?

- Would having a picture of that item be enough for me?

- Would I be comfortable leaving this to someone else to take care of?

- Why am I keeping this item?

- If no one else in my family wants this, why am I hanging on to it?

Gifts from loved ones are hard to part with, too, especially if the loved one has died. Even when they are given in love, these are just things. If they do not have space in the tiny home, or you do not want them because they aren't precious to you, donate them so someone else can enjoy the item.

When you ask these focused questions, it allows you to get deeper into the emotions and make some smart decisions about the sentimental items. Before you get rid of something sentimental, try giving it to a friend or family member. Tell them the story behind the item, where it came from, who gave it to you, why it is special. If they decide later that they don't want it, then that is fine too because you gave it to them, and it no longer belongs to you.

As we get older, we don't want our kids to have to deal with all our stuff after we die. That can be a very sad and emotional time for them. Help them now by getting rid of things you don't need so they don't have to. Don't expect your children to want your stuff, and you shouldn't make them feel guilty about that.

Remember, there are no U-Hauls behind a hearse, so you might as well start giving away the things now so you can tell them the stories that go with each item. Don't listen to the materialistic people that believe "whoever has the most toys when they die wins". It's just not true! It is not the things we have that are important; it is the memories and people in our lives that really matter.

In the past year, I have had two elderly ladies tell me that they grew up during the depression, and because of that, they have a really hard time getting rid of things. The problem is they now live with their children, and the home they now live in is no longer big enough for all the things they want to keep. I suggested to start giving away the items to family members now. If the family members don't want them, there is really no reason to keep hanging onto the items.

Donate What is Left

You will likely keep a couple of the sentimental items you have stored before moving into a small home. If you had boxes full of these items, narrowing it down to one or two is a great improvement. But what should you do with all the things you have decided not to keep?

Donating those items can be a good choice. This allows them to get a second life, rather than throwing them away in the trash and having them be gone forever. Donate the clothes and other items to a local shelter or donation center. If you have some antique things with historical value, then donate them to a local museum.

Chapter 6

Plan the Home

The first thing to consider is whether you would like to purchase or build a small home. This will depend on the current market in your location. Many markets have very low inventory and will not provide you with a ton of options when it comes to making a purchase, even for a small home. When this happens, it may be a good idea for you to investigate building your own small home. You can customize the home that best fits your family's needs and organize it to fit your lifestyle. If the market isn't as busy and you do see a small home for sale, it could save a lot of time buying that home rather than going through the long process of building a home.

There are so many decisions when building a home. It may get overwhelming going through the process if you work full time. Even looking at plans can get overwhelming! Do you want steps instead of a ladder (steps are easier to climb, and you can put drawers in each step, so none of the space is wasted), what fixtures do you want, what flooring, countertop, lighting, etc. Even a door's location can make a big difference in a tiny home. Usually buying an existing home is cheaper than building a new home. So many times when building you start out at one price, but by the time you are finished and have added all the bells and whistles, you have spent more than you should have.

In either case, you need to come up with a budget. Decide what you can afford and what will not stretch your budget too much. One of the reasons people will choose to go with a small home is to help maintain their budget.

One of the biggest considerations when picking out any type of home is to consider who will spend time in the home. This is true whether you choose a big or a small home. Some of the things to consider about the space you will need for other people in your life includes:

- How long do you expect your children to live with you? Even if they are in college, they may need to move back in. This does not mean you need to go with a big home, but maybe a spare bedroom or even some room in a finished basement can work.

- Do you have aging parents who may move in with you at some point? You can still live with them in a small home, but you may need to consider some of their medical needs or physical limitations. Do they need a walk-in shower, are there stairs, etc.?

- Do your children live far away? Having a little space for them to stay when they visit can be nice.

- How often do you plan to care for your grandchildren? You may not need a full room, but some space in the living room can be nice if they spend the night or still take naps.

- How often do you entertain houseguests? The more often you do this, the more room you will need.

How will you use your home for years to come? Do you plan to use the home as a workspace, now or in the future? Then you may want to find an office space or a nook where you can have a small desk, a computer, and some files.

Do you like to work out, and would you like to have some space for your exercise equipment? Do you plan to have animals who will need space to roam? Or maybe you do not plan to spend that much time at home because you will be traveling the world?

Having a good plan in place from the beginning can make a world of difference and help you pick out the right small home to serve your needs.

What do I need in a Small Home?

While some may choose to just go out and purchase the first small home they find, this is not a good home buying technique. You want to make sure that you can choose the right home that will be best for your needs, picking the one with the right layout, the right location, and other non-negotiables you want to have in your home before you spend all that money on a home. Sure, these smaller homes are less expensive than a big one, but it is still an important investment. Some of the things to consider when looking for your small home include:

- Assess what is non-negotiable: Think about some of the things that must be provided in a home you would like to purchase. Each homeowner will have their own list of non-negotiables, and you need to write a list before you get started. Do you need to have a certain number of bedrooms? Would you like to be in a certain neighborhood? Would you like to have a fireplace in the home?

- Pay attention to the square footage: Do not get into the trap of only looking at the square footage. This is a good starting point when looking at a home, but you do need to look at some of the different features that come with it. Look at some of the special things like granite countertops or high ceilings and compare those properties more than just their square footage.

- Give up on perfection: Too many homeowners will miss out on a good property because they are looking for perfection when they purchase their home. Perfection in a home is not possible, even if you decide to build the house instead. You can always change the home or make some updates that make the place your own once you move in. You do not need to settle for a home you don't like but having the idea that the home must be perfect can be bad.

- Look at the floor plan: It is easy to get caught up in all the home's finishes rather than in the functionality. The newest, nicest finishes are great, but they mean nothing if you do not like the home's flow. Updating things like the countertops and the paint will cost a lot less than trying to change the entire floor plan of the small home. Look around to see whether it is set up the way that you would like and make the other updates when you have time.

- Remember, a tall ceiling can make your tiny home feel much bigger on the inside. It will also give you more vertical wall space to work with. Going with a gable roof versus a flat roof is nice if you want some loft space for a bedroom or storage. Flat roofs can sometimes be more prone to leaking because the rain does not run off as easily.

- Waiting or choosing what is available: You do not need to jump on a home just because the market is tight. If you do not see yourself living in that home and making it your own, then it is good to step back, look at some of the other options, or just wait for a bit. There is nothing wrong with waiting for a better home to come up for sale rather than jumping into a home you do not like.

- Look at the neighborhood: You are not only picking out a home, but you are also buying the neighborhood. Take some time to look at the different neighborhoods you would like to purchase in to ensure they fit your needs. Realtors will tell you the most important thing about a home – location, location, location!

What's Your Goal for Your Small House?

Do you have the time and skills to do a fixer-upper home? Many times, you can purchase the home much cheaper if it needs some cosmetic improvements like paint, flooring, fixtures, etc.

Does the home need to be move-in ready? If you have small children, purchasing a safe home that has already had updates may be necessary because you may not have the time to do that while caring for children.

One way that you can be prepared for the change in the small home's space is to have a goal for what you would like to do. Maybe your goal is to decorate a room each month or do some repair work around the home to help increase the value and make the place more comfortable overall. Your goals can be as big or small as you can afford, based on what you would like to see accomplished in the home. Remember, your home is an investment, so you want to do things that will improve the asset. That includes keeping up with all the required maintenance in any size home.

Your goals can also be different based on whether you are a veteran homeowner or not. As a new homeowner, some of the goals you can make for the home include:

- Get some power tools to help you with a few DIY projects around the home

- Invest in some smart home upgrades

- Plan your landscaping both in the front and back yard. Perhaps that includes planting trees and shrubs

- Plan your outdoor living space

You can also advance this a bit the longer you stay in the home. You may take some time to minimize and get rid of some of the items you tend to leave all over the place and do not use as much. You could re-caulk the bathtub or paint the front door so that it is bright and sunny for those who come by. Think about upgrading some of the appliances depending on the age of the current devices in the home.

You need to create some goals for handling some of the work you want to do around your small home. Can you do the work yourself, or will you need to hire someone? Do you have a handyman you can rely on, or will you need to get some recommendations? Having a plan can help keep you motivated and make it more efficient to live in your small home.

Chapter 7

Choosing Furniture

Furnishing your new home can be an exciting time, no matter where you live. When you choose a small home, you may need to get a little more creative with the types of furniture that you prefer. You no longer have room for random furniture that doesn't serve a purpose, and you may find that it makes a lot of sense for you to go with furniture that can be used for more than one purpose.

Get rid of over-large furniture that takes up too much space and go for streamlined and sleek furniture that looks more modern and functional.

Homeowners of a small home will often choose their furniture based on how much they will use it. Coffee tables that have lift tops can double as a desk area. They make coffee tables now that can be lifted to three different heights to make them very versatile. Couches and chairs that convert to a bed and end tables with storage are all useful in your small home.

Keep the amount of furniture in your small home down to a minimum. It may be tempting to get that large hutch to show off the fancy China, but you likely do not have room for it. Pick out the minimum furniture that you need and keep your spaces open.

What to Know Before You Go Furniture Shopping

Furniture shopping can be a lot of fun. It gives you a chance to get out there and pick some of the items that you would like to enjoy in your home. There are so many brands and styles to choose from that you are certain to find the right one for you.

Before you jump right in and purchase the first item that you see, it is important to have a plan in place right from the start. This will help you pick out the items you want while saving space in your small home.

Measure the Room

Pull out a tape measure and write down all the dimensions for any room you plan to shop for. Be sure to mark the openings for all the doors and windows in the room. This will help you pick out furniture that will actually fit in that space. Take some pictures of the area too. This will help you visualize the space and figure out what will fit.

Research and Compare

Thanks to the internet, you can reach hundreds of furniture stores with a few mouse clicks. This will help you find the right item you need, no matter your style.

Take the time to shop online and see what is available. Look at some of the reviews for your chosen items, compare prices, and find some inspiration before you ever set foot in a store. This will help you be prepared and can keep you on task. There are so many pretty things in the stores that it is easy to get distracted from your goal!

Set a Budget

Once you walk into a furniture store, it is very easy to get caught up in all the details and fall in love with everything you see. This can quickly blow your budget and make you end up with way too much furniture for your small home.

Decide ahead of time how much you are willing to spend on that new room before you go shopping. You can choose to have a range, or just choose the maximum amount you are willing to spend on everything. Be careful about the financing deals offered. These can be utilized to save money, but only if you have a plan in place ahead of time and don't use it as an excuse to spend more than the budget.

Go for Quality, not Quantity

Instead of spending money on more furniture, consider spending money on high-quality furniture.

High-quality furniture may cost a little more to begin with, but it will quickly pay for itself in the length of time it will last. You can purchase a cheap couch lasting less than five years, leaving you having to buy a new one, or you can buy a couch that is a little more expensive that will last you for 20 years.

Take your time picking out the type of furniture that fits your style. Consider how long you would like it to last, where it will fit, and how it goes with your current lifestyle. This will help you to get the right furniture for your small home. If you have pets and/or children, be sure to pick a fabric that is easy to clean.

Versatile Furniture

You need to get really creative at utilizing every inch of space. Many companies are starting to catch on to the trend of small homes and are happy to create some of the products you need. See

https://www.wayfair.com/furniture/cat/small-space-living-rooms-c1867351.html

Is the item foldable, like a fold-up desk needed only a couple of times a week? Fold-up tables and chairs are great for extra guests. Remember, versatility is the key to buying furniture for a small space. This can free up a lot of room in your home while still giving you a comfortable place to sit and relax.

All furniture needs to have a dual purpose. Many coffee tables will come with drawers or can even open to allow pillows and blankets to go inside to keep things tidy. Consider putting the coffee table on wheels. When not in use it can easily be pushed out of the way. Another thing to consider is how to utilize your current coffee table. If you do not have it in the budget to purchase another one, you can add a few storage cubes or bins to slide under the table, which hold the items you need to keep.

Some couches will have storage drawers in them where you can store books, pillows, and blankets, so they are out of the way and still readily accessible if you need them. Consider how you can get your furniture involved in the storage to help you get the most out of each space.

I would not recommend furniture that is built in. It will be harder to replace, and you can't move it around. It may be a necessity if you are planning on living in an RV or a liveaboard boat, but if not, try and get quality furniture that you can change as your needs change and that is easier to fit the space.

Instead of wasting space with an end table and a floor lamp, purchasing a floor lamp with an attachable small table is possible. You can get the light you need while also having a small area to put down your books, keys, and other items you need at that time, without taking up any more room than the lamp itself.

When you are picking out furniture for your small space, there are a few things to consider in order to get the most room. Some of these include:

- Keep it skinny: This is not the place for the big puffy couches. They may look neat and feel comfortable, but they take up a lot of space that you do not have.

- Use the corners: Pick out items that can go nicely against the corners and edges in the room to keep the middle free and clear.

- Only pick pieces with storage like end tables, ottomans, etc.

- Pull double duty: Pieces like a hide-a-bed can work well in a small home. They may be your couch during the morning but turn into a bed you need at night or when guests come over to visit.

- Bookshelves that will turn into a desk or table area are a great use of space.

Some of the versatile items may be more expensive, but since they work as two or three pieces of furniture at once, you are still getting a great deal on them.

Versatile Appliances

Even stackable washers and dryers can take up a tiny home's space. They also make washing machines that can become dryers too. It takes more time to get the laundry completed, but you have everything you need in one machine. You don't always have to use the dryer; many people prefer to hang clothes up to dry or outside when the weather is nice.

Tiny homes' kitchens are usually small, so instead of a full-size oven, you can purchase a toaster oven and a microwave that can be set on shelves in the kitchen and take up far less space. If you get a smooth stove top, you can also use it for countertop space when not using the burners.

You may decide you do not need a full-size refrigerator. You can find smaller apartment-size fridges to save some space. If the refrigerator is shorter than normal, build some drawers to set it on top of to make it taller and easier to access. This also creates more storage space under the refrigerator.

Consider the Delivery Details

Unless you have a large moving van available, you will most likely need to get the new furniture delivered to your small home. Make sure to check with the store on their delivery options. Some questions to ask ahead of time include:

- What is the exact time of delivery? See if they will provide you with more details than just a date and a large range of times.

This helps assure you can be home at delivery time. Many companies will call you an hour or so before they plan to drop the item off.

- Will I need to move the furniture myself? If the answer is yes, you will need to call in some help to get the work done. Furniture sliders are a must-have when you have large furniture to move around. They are inexpensive, and they sell sliders for both carpet and tile/vinyl/hardwood floors.

- Will I need to assemble the furniture myself? Many stores offer full-service delivery, which means they will do the assembly for you, but always check on this.

Check into the costs for delivering the items as well. Some will provide this for free; some may have conditions on how much you need to spend, how many miles you are from the store, or the item's weight to get it for free. Others will charge either way. Ask for the costs and add these into the budget for the item(s) you want to purchase.

Chapter 8

Maximizing Your Space

You need to get smart about the space available in the home and take the necessary steps to ensure you utilize it all. Learning how to maximize your space can make the tiny house feel more like home without all the clutter or feeling cramped.

What is Vertical Space in a Home?

The amount of space you have on the floors and at eye level will be limited. When you take the time to use your vertical space, you will find more room on the walls of the small home than you originally imagined.

Vertical space is all that space from the home floors to the ceilings. Much of this will often go under-utilized because homeowners will not think about using this space for their needs. By stacking, sorting, and using shelving, you can add a lot more space to your tiny home.

Whenever possible, look for a small or tiny home with high ceilings. This makes a small room feel much larger. Plus, it can give you a lot of vertical space to work with.

A few ideas for vertical space-

-Small toys such as cars and trucks are great stored on shallow picture ledges on the wall of your child's bedroom.

-If the side and/or front of your fridge is exposed, put magnetic shelves on the fridge or hooks to hold often used kitchen items such as hot pads, oils or vitamins.

-Pegboards are not only great in the garage, but they also come in handy over a desk as they can hold office supplies, scissors, craft items, etc.

-Put small command hooks on your wall in your closet to hold jewelry. Larger hooks can also be used to hold purses, scarves, ties, and belts.

-Put nets in the corners of children's bedrooms to hold the stuffed animals.

Since many tiny homes are just as tall as traditional homes, even if they are smaller, there is a lot of potential for storage when you choose to go up. Utilize unique storage options such as shelves above the doors and windows to help store books, photo albums and other items that you would like to keep in your tiny home.

How to Create Vertical Storage Space with Design

While you do not want just to stack a ton of junk against the walls and call it good, there are some options that you can utilize to make use of the vertical space in that area.

For example, are you a fan of having a nice cup of tea at night or need a few cups of coffee to get you up and going in the morning? Coffee and teacups can take up a lot of space in your kitchen cupboards. Instead of wasting that space, consider making a hanging design on the wall. You can put them back up when you are done with your tea and have easy access anytime you need them.

Create a cute design on your kitchen wall with your favorite hot pads. Put your tea or coffee in pretty containers to put on shelves. Hang your plants on the wall and create a design.

Use both sides of your shelves. If the shelf is in the kitchen, screw the metal lids from spice jars to the underside or bottom of the shelf to keep them handy.

Clear plastic stackable drawers are a great option. With a few containers, you can really maximize the space in your closet. Put some in the kids' room to contain their toys for easy access. Use them in the pantry to store food or other items. They come in several sizes, and you can stack two or three together. You can also continue to add more if needed.

Other tips to help you maximize the storage space in your tiny home include:

- The side of the counter: Stop letting cookbooks and other important items take up space on the counter. Add a little storage rack to the side to keep things organized without wasting that valuable counter space.

- Double up under the sink: Just by adding a bar or another similar item under the sink, you can double the space by hanging the cleaning supply bottles on the bar. This frees up the bottom of the cabinet for other things.

- Use the backs of doors. Put a shoe organizer on your closet door or a toy organizer for your kids. These are also great to put on the back of doors in bathrooms to hold a lot of toiletries.

- Attach a file holder to the wall or cabinet to hold your cutting boards to keep them all in one place.

- Add the hooks: You can put hooks in almost any place in the home to give you more storage. A few hooks in the bathroom provide an instant place to store the towels. Hooks near the door are handy to hang up keys, hats, and umbrellas.

- Move the furniture up: A loft may be a good option if you are in a truly tiny home. This allows you to put your bedroom up and out of the way while utilizing the rest of your home for entertaining and family time.

Maximizing Ceiling Storage

You can utilize your ceilings to make something creative. Many options work here including hooks, a cargo net, slings, a pulley system, and overhead racks.

When choosing the right storage for your ceilings, go with something high-quality. You do not want to add things to hooks and shelves and then have everything fall on top of you. This is not a place to skimp on the work you do in your home, so go with ones covered by warranty and made from quality material so they will last. You may want to see about having a professional put the heavy storage racks together for you. This can be done when you build the tiny home or can be added later.

The ceiling is a good location to put items that you do not want to get rid of but won't use all that often. Camping supplies, extra pillows and linens for guests, and summer and winter clothes can all be stored on the ceiling during the off-season. Also, holiday items you only need once a year. This keeps them out of the way yet easy enough to access when you need them.

A pulley system could be used to allow you to maximize the ceiling space and still give you easy access to the stored item above your head.

Using the Awkward Nooks to Your Advantage

Your tiny home may have a few awkward nooks that you need to pay attention to. Ignoring these points and not taking advantage of them will result in a lot of wasted space in a home that does not have a lot of space to start with.

The first step is to make it into a custom storage area. Whether the nook is small or tall, you can put it to use as a unique storage area. You can find some custom wall-mounted floating shelves to suit your space or even some organizational units or standalone shelves and hooks.

Another option is to use that space to create a mini gallery. This can turn it into something aesthetically pleasing, especially if that nook is in an area not used often. You can hang up some of your framed art or pictures or arrange some books on a skinny shelf to dress up the area.

If you have one of these awkward nooks right near the door, turn it into a landing zone for when you walk in the door. A console table may be able to fit there or some hooks to hold your keys and the mail. This area may not be able to have a coat stand, but even a small space can work to keep things organized.

Do you plan to work at home in a small home? Then utilize one of these nooks as your new home office. You do not need to have a huge area to do this. A shelving unit attached to the wall with a few boxes for storage above it can help you contain paper, pens, and office supplies while giving you room to write things down and even an area for your laptop.

You often need less space for some of those big dreams you have. Setting something up even in the smallest areas will help you better utilize the space.

How to Find More Space in Your Small Home

Some of the different options you can use to free up some more space in your small home include:

- Get furniture with the legs exposed to make the room seem bigger. You can also store flat items under a sofa or large chair

- Mount the television on the wall rather than getting a bulky entertainment system

- Keep things in neutral colors to lighten up the area and make it seem bigger

- Build strategic storage and really think about the point of use for an item to be sure it is where you will need to use it

- Pick a big rug to help the eyes widen around the space

- Use the space around and over the toilet in the bathroom. Over-the-toilet storage cabinets are a great solution and easy to install.

- Consider a pocket door to aid in privacy while ensuring you do not waste space in the hallways and rooms.

- If you have a loft with stairs, be sure and use the space under the stairs and the stairs themselves. Drawers can be put in each step to help store items.

The trick here is to plan everything out. A home can be a lot smaller than you may imagine, but you need to make all the nooks and crannies fit the items you need. No matter how much you downsize your home, there are still basic items you need when living in the home. Being smart about some of the things you bring in and planning out the limited space you have can make a big difference in how much you can fit into each space.

Chapter 9

The Decoration Guide

Some simple decorations can make the home feel more like it belongs to you and can really add to your comfort level. You will need to use slightly different techniques when decorating a tiny home compared to a big one to ensure the space looks good and you can use the limited space you have.

Types of Décor for Small Homes

Remove any extra accent pieces from the shelves and keep the decorations down to a minimum. Items need to have a "home" within your home. Letting things lay around will really cramp up the limited space.

In the kitchen, you can have some simple white walls with open upper shelving to help expand the eyes up in the tiny kitchen. Wooden shelves that have live edges add texture and interest. Splashes of color can be fun, too, for accent walls.

Wallpaper can be your friend in a tiny home. It allows you to add some bright colors and patterns to any room without taking up more space. Plus, it is much easier to add in some of the patterns you want than tile, which could be expensive to change later when you are tired of it. Go with something simple or elegant, bright, bold, or muted based on your style preferences.

The Peel and Stick Tiles can really add some texture and design to a kitchen backsplash or on the bathroom wall. They are easy and far less expensive than installing regular tile. They can completely change the look of your kitchen or bathroom in minutes. There are many styles to choose from, and they can be found online or at Lowes stores. Our houseboat had very dark paneling in the kitchen. We couldn't have used regular tiles because they would have been too heavy and too wide to put under the small kitchen window. The peel and stick tiles were perfect. They brightened up the space, they are easy to clean, and we received many compliments on how nice they looked.

Even your furniture can turn into a décor style choice for your home. Choose a built-in cabinet that can hold your books and pictures and even has a space for your bar service when guests come to visit. Add some decorative mirrors to some of the walls in your living and dining room to help brighten up the area and give it the appearance of having more space.

If you have any collectibles, try to use them to decorate so you can enjoy your collection instead of just being stored in a closet. Use stagger shelving: Uniform shelving can overpower a smaller room. A ladder-style piece as a shelf will look better and not be overwhelming.

Always remember that light is your best friend. Light can open up any room, whether it is big or small. In a small space, let in the light as much as possible. Adding a mirror opposite your windows can help to open the space.

For bathrooms, to keep the privacy but still let the light in the windows, you can attach the peel and stick clear frosted contact paper to the window. If you get tired of it, you can always pull it back off.

Replacing doors with sliding walls in large doorways can make your space feel much larger. This works really well on patio doors to make the inside and outside flow together.

Choosing the Right Rug for a Small Home

An area rug can be a great decision for someone who lives in a small home. It allows you to show off your hardwood floors while giving some softness and comfort to the room. When used properly, it can naturally define different spaces in the living room without needing more furniture or walls, and it is easier to remove. A decorative rug can brighten up any room of your home.

The first thing to consider when picking out an area rug is the size you will need. You do not want the rug to be too small, or it just looks like a floor mat-but you may be limited on space too. Before you start shopping, measure the space in the room and decide how much you would like covered up with the rug. Some of the standard sizes you can choose from include:

- 6 by 9 feet

- 8 by 10 feet

- 9 by 12 feet

- 10 by 14 feet

If your space is smaller than some of the standard sizes, you can choose to get a custom-size rug. A good rule of thumb is to choose between four to eight inches of bare floor on each side of the rug.

Then it is time to choose the rug's color and pattern. A patterned rug can help add interest and color to the room if you need more variety there, but a solid-colored rug will blend in better if the room is already eclectic. You can pull one or two colors from the décor in the rest of the room and then choose them as the hues for your rug to make sure it matches well.

With the size and color chosen, it is time to look at the material and texture. Think about how you would like the rug to feel when you step on it. Wool, cotton, synthetics, viscose, and acrylic are materials commonly found in area rugs. These can all look nice and are easy to clean.

If you want to divide the room into several areas, you can get more than one rug to allow for this. Or it is possible to get one large rug to help centralize and give you a simple piece to pull the whole room together.

Choosing Flowers and Plants

One simple way to decorate your home is with flowers and plants. These can be beautiful and are easy to change out with the seasons without taking up a lot of space. Choosing the right flowers can bring the whole décor of your tiny home together. To help you choose the right flowers, consider the following:

Flowers for Spaces without Light

You can add some flowers to the corridors and halls in your home, but these areas do not have a lot of light. It can be hard to find a flower that will thrive in such spaces. These areas will do well with calatheas, sansevierias, and bromeliads. Bathrooms can lack natural light too, and with the high humidity, you need to choose something like an anthurium or orchid to spruce up that area.

Decorate the Kitchen with Plants

Consider using herbal plants for your kitchen area. This helps you have some of the herbs and spices you need in medicine and cooking while making your kitchen look fresh and beautiful. Mint, basil, rosemary, and parsley are great for this area. Just make sure to place them in the sunlight for a good portion of the day.

Choosing Plants for Spaces with Lots of Light

Bright rooms open up a lot of potential for the space and allow for more decorative possibilities. In very bright rooms, introduce just a hint of color and contrast with some fresh flowers. Gerberas are good for this setting, or red roses can be nice. If you want to add a plant to your home instead of a flower, go with a Swiss cheese plant, corn plant, or a calathea.

Choosing Curtains

Choosing the right color and fabric for curtains can help brighten a room and give you the necessary privacy when they are closed. The material you choose will play a big role in the look of the curtains. You can choose lightweight cotton, sheer lace, or heavy fabric to change the look. To help you pick the right fabric, you must consider:

How much sunlight would you like in the room? Heavier fabrics are best for traditional rooms, and sheer fabrics are good for minimalistic rooms with more light.

Sheers are best for a tiny home. These can let more light in, which really opens a space. Heavier materials may feel luxurious but can make it feel like the walls are closing in.

The color is important to consider too. The color of your curtains should match the furniture in the room. You can choose colors that harmonize with the décor or ones that contrast but have a plan. Lighter colors are best for tiny homes because they can open up the space.

Patterns can be a good option for some homes, but do not make the patterns too bold or busy. These can overpower the room and may make it feel even smaller. Plain colors or simple patterns will work best in your small home.

While it may seem counterintuitive, you may find that longer curtains work best for your tiny home. Longer curtains tend to draw the eye up and down, which can make the room look larger than normal. Pick floor-to-ceiling curtains for the best results.

Lighting Your Small Space

The more light you can add to your space in a tiny home, the more open it can feel. When the space seems dark, or you only choose a few lighting sources, it can really ruin the appearance and make your space feel smaller. Adding many lights in the home, especially to the room's corners, can make the space feel bigger.

There are different ways you can add light to your home. Choosing a lamp that can double as a work of art is a great idea for this smaller space. Many decorative lamps can fit on your end table, hang from the ceiling, or connect to the walls to add a decorative touch to any room in the home while brightening it up.

A unique option to try is a multi-directional chandelier. This is a dynamic choice that can shine light around the small room. It works great in rooms that do not have a lot of natural light or those that are naturally smaller and need light to brighten them up.

Since you can only add so many lights to your tiny home, it may be good to add a few mirrors into a room that struggles to stay light. Mirrors can double the lighting effects of any room while only taking up a minimal amount of space. Large, elegant mirrors can add a classic touch and will really brighten the room.

How the Light Impacts the Perception of Your Home

Not only can light make your home look bigger, which is imperative in a tiny home, but poor lighting can also affect many aspects of your health. Homes with poor lighting can be detrimental to your visual performance, your safety, and physiological functions.

When a room does not have enough light, it is hard to see. This can

make it a challenge to do daily tasks around the home and can harm your safety. If you can't see what is around you while walking through the home, it is easy to fall and sustain an injury. Adding more light can help prevent these injuries and falls.

Light can also play a critical role in your endocrine and nervous systems and can even affect the secretion of hormones including melatonin. Melatonin is released based on how much light is present and will regulate the body's circadian rhythm. This hormone is highest at night when it is dark out and lowest during the day when we need to be awake. With poor lighting in the home, this rhythm can be affected.

Things Never to Do When Designing the Interior of a Small Home

While we have discussed a lot of design ideas you can do to help your small space, there are also things you need to avoid when it comes to this tiny living arrangement. Some of the decorating mistakes that you should avoid include:

· Interrupting the visual flow: When the home has many small adjacent rooms together, you can make the space feel bigger by visually connecting the rooms. This can be done with a similar style, material type, or color palette. Flooring is important in this area. If the flooring is all the same, this can really help with the room's continuity and allow the space to flow better.

· Fighting the size: Don't try to force your small size to become a big size. If you do not have room for some decorations or a type of furniture, then do not try to add these to the space. This can cramp the space and will make you miserable.

· Choosing the wrong bed size: In a tiny home, a four-poster bed could take up too much space. You can still have a nice headboard without crowding the room. You just need to get creative here. The headboard could be attached to the wall so as not to take up any extra space. A captain's bed with drawer storage can give you the needed storage space. Putting your bed on a raiser can also give you extra storage by allowing you to store more items under the bed. The headboard can also double as a bookshelf if you love to read, and it is a good use of the space.

. Having closed-in arrangements: While you may be limited on space, you will feel better if you have some airflow around items in the home. When furniture and other items are on top of each other, it can feel hard to breathe.

· Choosing dark colors: Dark colors can be fun, but bright and light colors are better for a small home. Light colors can add a lot of personality to the walls while also making the room feel bigger.

· Overusing small furniture; Just because the furniture is small does not mean that you must purchase it. Unless you have the space for the item and know how you will use it, keep it out of your home.

Decorating a tiny home takes a bit more creativity, but you can do it!

Chapter 10

What to Know When Buying a Small House

You have decided to purchase a small home. This is a big step into the financial freedom you deserve and a minimalist life that allows you to focus on the more important things in life. Before you jump feet first into purchasing this small home, let's look at some of the things that you need to know when it is time to buy a small home.

Pictured is an example of some of the tiny home floor plans. This can also give you an idea of how you can tow the different sizes of tiny homes. See www.TinyHouseDesign.com for more information.

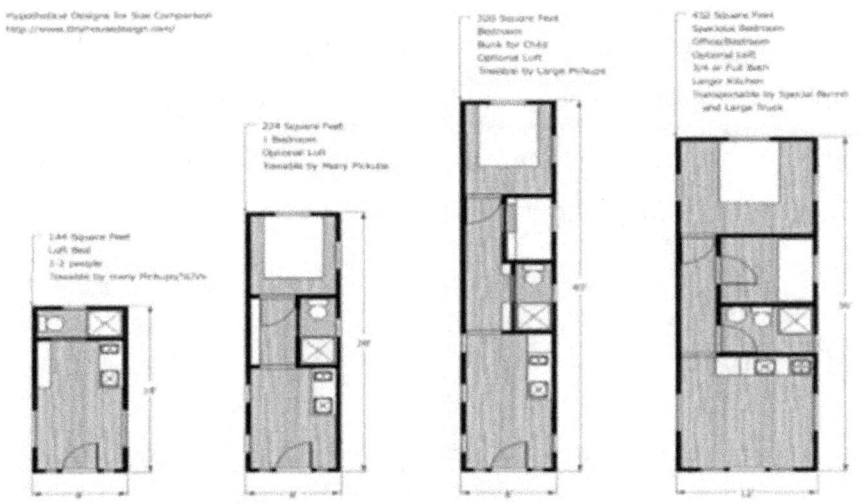

Tips for First Time Home Buyers

Purchasing a tiny home can be a great experience, especially if you have never been a homeowner before, but the process can be overwhelming. It can take more time than many first-time buyers are willing to sacrifice. You need to find a lender who will pre-approve your loan (not all will be comfortable lending money for a tiny home), then you need to find the home, get an offer accepted, and go through the mortgage process.

Knowing where to start can be the hardest part. Some of the tips to remember as you prepare to purchase your tiny home include:

Know Your Credit

All lenders will look at your credit score. This helps them see whether you are consistent at making on-time payments and how much debt you have concerning your income. If your credit score is low or you have some problem areas, fix these before you decide to apply for a mortgage. The higher your credit score, the better the interest rate you will achieve on your mortgage. If you can get your credit score to over 700, it may allow you to get a lower interest rate on the mortgage.

Set a Budget

Never look at any type of home without setting a budget. Review your finances and determine what you would be most comfortable with concerning monthly payments. Even tiny and small homes can get expensive, so have that number in mind. The number you like may not be the same as what the bank will give you, so be prepared.

While each lender will have their own calculators to determine how much to loan, here are some good guidelines:

· Debt free: If you have no debts when purchasing the home, you can consider homes five times your yearly income.

· If 20% or less of your income goes to debt, you can shop for a home four times your yearly income.

· If more than 20% of your income goes to debt, you can afford a home three times your yearly income or less.

It is best to talk to your lender to get a more accurate amount for the home price you can afford.

Most sellers will not accept an offer from you until you are pre-approved, so talk to mortgage lenders first.

Start Saving for the Down Payment

You must have some kind of down payment to get a loan. While traditional homes can offer programs that allow 5% or less down, this is less common with a tiny home. You may need to have at least 20% down to do a non-traditional home. Start saving in advance, so you have the money ready for purchase.

As you save for the down payment, consider the other costs you should save for the home. This includes property taxes and insurance (which are often rolled into the mortgage payment), utilities, maintenance, moving expenses and more.

Compare Rates from More Than One Lender

As you work on getting pre-approval from the bank, compare more than one lender. Each lender has different rules they need to follow, and you may be able to get a better rate from one lender over another. Get quotes from at least three different lenders and compare the interest rate, total loan costs, additional fees, and annual percentage rates.

Keep Your Credit Stable

Once you apply for your mortgage, your credit needs to stay frozen. Do not open any new accounts, rack up credit card debt, or do anything that will change your finances. Doing so may jeopardize your mortgage, and you may lose out on the home. Your lender will check the credit score several times during the process, including right before closing, and will catch any new debt, and that could jeopardize your loan.

Don't Empty the Bank Account

While there are many upfront costs of purchasing a home, you should not empty your bank account to pay for them. This is risky and will leave you with nothing if unexpected expenses come up. Try to save extra money meant for moving or purchasing the home to help you be prepared.

Find a Good Inspector

Even when purchasing a tiny home, you must have a home inspection. If anything major is wrong with the home, you can ask the seller to fix it, give you a credit to fix it yourself, or walk away from the property. This provides you with the protection you need to get a complete property inspection.

Some of the major items (and expensive to fix) included in the inspection are leaky pipes (resulting in water damage), failing water heaters, heating and air conditioning problems, foundation cracks, and sewer system problems. If the inspector finds any of these major issues, you need to go back to the seller and negotiate.

How to Buy Tiny Houses

There are several places where you can purchase a tiny home on wheels if you would like to have a mobile life and see the world. Some options include:

- **Amazon:** The online retail giant Amazon does have some prefabricated tiny homes you can purchase. These will come with most of the materials you need outside the foundation and roof. You will need to bring in professionals to help put it together and meet local codes, and you must have land on which to place the home.

· **Realtor.com:** This is a good place to begin your search for pre-owned tiny homes in your area. You can also contact realtors on that site to see whether they know of potential properties coming up for sale.

· **Sprout Tiny Homes:** The Sprout Tiny Homes community is found in two towns in Colorado. These are planned communities that come with tiny homes for you to purchase.

· **Tumbleweed Tiny House Company:** This company allows you to purchase a tiny home on wheels that is certified green. There are many models and floor plans for you to choose from.

The certified green designation includes – energy-efficient appliances and lighting, efficient heating and air conditioning, composting toilets, and dual pane energy-efficient windows.

Tiny House Listings and Tiny House Marketplace are also two good options that allow you to search for tiny homes for sale based on your location, your budget, and the exact specifications for your new home. You can also talk to local contractors to see whether they will build a tiny home for you if none are available for sale.

Choosing a Realtor for a Small House

A real estate agent can make a lot of sense for those who want to purchase a tiny home and need someone in their corner along the way. Purchasing a home, especially if it is your first one, can be daunting. There are inspections to set up, appraisers to listen to, and negotiations to win to get your home. Rather than doing this yourself, you can work with an experienced realtor to make it easier.

The right realtor will walk you through the process of purchasing a home. They can answer questions, help you look at homes that meet your budget and even write out the most attractive offer to get you noticed. Once the contracts are signed, they will be there to schedule the appraiser, the inspections, and help through any challenge that comes along until the keys are in your hand. And since the seller pays the commissions for the agent, it makes sense to have this professional there to help you.

The biggest challenge is figuring out how to choose the right real estate agent for your needs. Some tips to help you make this important decision include:

· **Compare agents online:** Use an agent finder tool to help you vet local agents and find the right one. Compare several agents to see who may have experience buying and selling tiny homes.

· **Get a referral:** There is nothing better than getting a personal referral from someone you know.

· **Meet the agents:** Meet three or more agents to see who may be best suited to help you with your purchase. Never settle for the first agent you meet. Ask each agent the same questions to get a feel of who can handle your home buying process.

· **Ask the right questions:** There are many questions you can ask your realtor before hiring them. The more questions you ask, the easier it is to pick one who will work hard for you. Some questions to ask include:

o How much experience do you have in real estate?

o Do you work mostly with sellers or buyers?

o How many clients do you take on at a time?

o What is your specialty?

o Do you have experience purchasing small or tiny homes?

o Do you have at least three references you can give me?

o Are you part of a team?

o Do you work part-time or full-time as a realtor?

· **Have a communication preference:** Talk to the agent about how they will contact you. If you like emails because you are at work and the agent only does phone calls, this may not be a good fit. You also want someone who will get back to you quickly. While agents can be busy with other clients and won't respond immediately all the time, you do not want to wait days to hear back during the buying process.

There are many great realtors and real estate companies around the country. But you need to take the time to pick the realtor who has a good understanding of the tiny home market and will advocate for you through every step of the process.

Considering Affordability and Total Costs

Considering the affordability of a home before purchasing can be an important step when getting a tiny home. You need to consider your income, any debts, and your savings amount. Purchasing a home is a big financial decision, and you want to make sure that you pick out a home that is affordable on your budget, even if it is a tiny or small home.

One metric that a lender will use to determine whether a home is affordable for you is to calculate the debt-to-income ratio. The DTI (Debt to Income) ratio will compare your total monthly debts (including the estimated amount of the new mortgage) to your monthly pre-tax income. Your credit score can help you qualify for a higher ratio, but most lenders want your housing expenses to stay at or below 28% of your monthly income.

We can look at an example of this. If your monthly mortgage payment, with insurance and taxes, is $1260 a month, you would need to make $4500 a month before taxes to keep the DTI ratio at 28%. You can take this the other way to see the ideal housing budget. Just take your income and multiply it by 0.028. This will give you the total amount of housing costs you should be able to afford. Of course, the lower the DTI, the more affordable the home.

The DTI ratio of 0.28% just relates to your overall housing payment. Lenders will also look at your current debts. Most will not want your total debts, including your mortgage, to be more than 26% of your monthly income. This gives you money left for daily living expenses on top of owning the home.

Always include the total cost of the mortgage when running the numbers. The mortgage and insurance will just be part of the equation. If you can't put the full 20% down, you will also need to pay PMI (Private Mortgage Insurance) as a security for the lender. This insurance is very expensive, and you should try and get the loan down as quickly as possible to avoid paying PMI. If possible, every month, pay extra on the principal of your mortgage. It can save years on the loan and help you pay it off much faster. There are also costs for taxes, insurance, and HOA (Homeowner Association). These must be factored into the total mortgage amount when determining the DTI.

All lenders will look at your debt and income differently. Some of the key factors that lenders will consider when checking the affordability of your home include your monthly income, your cash reserves to help with the down payment and closing costs, your credit profile, and your monthly expenses. In inflationary times, interest rates on a mortgage start to increase. Be sure you can afford increased monthly payments if you cannot lock in a lower interest rate and they jump up before your closing. Never get in over your head; it is just too stressful.

Closing Costs on Your Home

Besides the 20% down payment, lenders will charge other fees for their services. Lender fees can be between 1 to 3% of the home's total cost, and these are called points. It is sometimes possible to negotiate these down. You will also need to pay for an inspector, appraisal costs, and any additional points purchased to lower your interest rate.

Talk to your lender early on to estimate how much your closing costs will be. These numbers can change the closer you get to the closing date, but they can give you a good idea of how much money you must allocate. Some sellers will offer to pay for these closing costs in a strong buyers' market, but this is less common in a seller's market.

Get the Insurance Right

When purchasing a home, you must choose homeowner's insurance. Your mortgage lender will not give you the loan without having a policy in place. As a first-time homebuyer, you may feel overwhelmed by all the available policies. While the price is important, the amount of coverage, the claims process, and other factors need to be considered.

Homeowner's insurance is important for your protection. Some of the steps include:

What Coverage You Need

You must get several quotes from more than one company to help you compare coverage and prices. As you do this, you need to get an exact calculation of the coverage amount you need. Getting too much or too little coverage will change the amount you pay for the policy. Consider getting an estimate of the following:

·   **The home's replacement cost:** The insurance coverage you receive on the home should be equal to the amount it would cost you to replace it if it were destroyed by fire, windstorm, flooding, etc. Insurers can often provide their own cost estimate for this with their online estimate tools, or you can hire a professional appraiser to help.

·   **The value of your personal belongings:** You need enough coverage to help cover the value of your personal items if something happens to the home.

·   **The value of your assets:** pick a policy with enough personal liability coverage to cover your net worth in case someone gets hurt on your property and you get sued.

The amount of coverage you need depends on the location of your home too. Some homes may need extra coverage for hurricanes or flooding. Check with your lender to see what they require.

Gather Information About Your Home

To help you get an accurate quote on your home insurance, you will need to provide the insurance company with information on the home. Gather the information ahead of time to make this process easier. Some information you will need include:

·   The square footage of the home and the type of roof. They will also need to know the age of the roof.

·   The heating method of your home, whether it is electric or gas.

·   Any information on the home's renovation history.

·   Whether the home has a pool, a trampoline, or pets.

·   Whether this is your second or primary home.

·   Are you going to live in the home or rent it out?

The more details you can provide to the insurance company, the more accurate your quote.

Compare Quotes

Always compare rates between three or more companies before choosing a policy. This helps you compare coverage and prices to get the best deal. Don't pick a company just because they have the least expensive rates. This could leave large gaps in your coverage and may leave you open to more risks.

Pay attention to the quotes you get from any insurance company. Look to see not only the rate they offer, but the exact amount of coverage they will provide. You want a balance between full coverage and the price that you pay. Check with your mortgage lender to see if they have any coverage requirements before distributing the loan.

Choose Your Policy

After comparing quotes, it is time to select a policy and customize it to suit your coverage needs. You can add some endorsements to the policy at an additional cost if you need them. Some common endorsements that you can choose include:

- Earthquake coverage

- Flood coverage

- Guaranteed replacement cost

- Extended replacement cost

- Scheduled personal property coverage

- Service line coverage

- Appliance breakdown coverage

- Water backup coverage

You may not be required to have these endorsements, so it will be a personal choice whether you would like to include them.

Finalize Policy Details

At this point, you have compared the quotes, gotten your questions answered, and selected the policy. You will need to schedule the home inspection too. Then it is time to finalize a few policy details before closing on the home. These details include:

- **Choose the deductible:** You will need to set the deductible for your policy. This is the amount of money you will need to cover on each claim before the insurance pays anything. A higher deductible can lower the premium. This means you will pay more out of pocket each time something happens to the home.

- **Determine how the premiums are paid:** Most lenders will ask you to bring a full year of premiums for the insurance to closing. You will then pay a portion of the premium each month with your payment, so it is ready for the next year. This can be done in the same escrow account as your property taxes.

· **Set your policy dates:** You will be able to choose the policy period, which is when the insurance begins and ends. Make sure that you have coverage on the day you move into the home.

I would be very grateful if you would leave a review for

The Small Living Guide for Compact Houses

on Amazon!

Chapter 11

More Secrets to Living in a Small Home

Living in a small home can be a great experience. It opens many doors that are not available with living in a big home. It takes some time to adjust to living in a smaller space, but when you learn how to make any home more efficient, you will find that it can improve your life experiences.

Material Resources

The Habitat for Humanity ReStore Stores are all over the United States. They can be a great resource for recycled building supplies. We bought a home that had a broken tank lid on the back of the toilet. They had tried to glue it back together, but it looked really bad. The rest of the toilet was in perfect shape, so we didn't want to take the time and expense of replacing the entire toilet. We took the broken lid to our local ReStore store to find a match. They had 100s of tank lids, and we found the exact match for only $5! We have several stores in the cities around us, and they all stock different materials. Some have lots of new flooring still in the box; some have furniture, tile, and bathtubs. Most stock kitchen cabinets, windows, doors, lighting, and tools. Using recycled materials can bring a lot of character into a home with rustic barn doors, live edge countertops, etc. If you decide to do a fixer-upper or just want to rehab some areas in your home, you can do it much cheaper by using recycled materials!

This is from their website - *Whether you are a do-it-yourselfer, homeowner, renter, landlord, contractor, interior designer, environmentalist, or treasure hunter, make Habitat for Humanity ReStore your first stop when shopping for your next home improvement, renovation, or DIY project. There are hundreds of ReStore locations – and they're all open to the public. Find a Habitat ReStore near you.* https://www.habitat.org/restores

Off The Grid

A small home can be a great way to move off-grid and enjoy a more sustainable lifestyle without all the trappings of modern life. Maybe you just want to be kinder to the world we live in. There are many ways that you can make your small home more self-sufficient.

We all need to do our part to reduce, reuse, repurpose, and recycle.

Once you are done with an item in your home, consider whether you can reuse it. You may need to get creative such as an empty jar now becoming a candle holder or drinking glass.

Water

The first thing to consider is your water collection system. A good potable water source is so important when you want to live off-grid. Living off-grid means you may not have access to the municipal county or city water sources, and you will need to choose how to get water. Pick out an area that either comes with a natural water source or is convenient for you to haul water.

Along the same lines, you will need to have a water collection system. A rain barrel attached to a gutter can be a good method. You can make it as simple or complex as you want, but a water collection system will help you have fresh water whenever it rains. It can be used for washing and watering the lawn and your plants. If you set up the correct water filtering system, you can even drink the water. Don't let the precious rainwater go to waste.

Food

The next thing to consider is the food you will eat. You can still head to the grocery store occasionally but living off-grid means you will need to grow a lot of your own food in a garden or a greenhouse, making your tiny home more sustainable. This activity is good for the land and can provide you and your family with the healthy foods you need. Plus, it can save you money while making delicious meals.

You can produce meat and eggs on your homestead as well. A few chickens are a good place to start. A chicken coop doesn't take up much space on the land and is quick to build. If you start to get too many eggs or chickens, you can always trade with someone else for other items like milk, meat, cheeses, etc. You may want to consider learning how to preserve the food, too, if you live in an area with long winters to make sure you have food when the weather turns difficult.

Build a composting box: Composting is a great way to help conserve your resources. You can turn your food leftovers and lawn debris into a rich soil used in your garden to grow your food.

Power Generation System

You need to consider your off-grid power. You will not be connected to the power grid, so you will need to find a way to generate your own electricity to have lights, heat, and other power. You need a power generating system with backups to provide you with the required electricity. Even small steps are enough to help your energy consumption. Consider turning the thermostat down a few degrees to save money, wash your clothes in cold water, and keep the water heater at a lower temperature to help sustain your home. A tankless water heater can save you a lot of closet space too.

For most small homes off-grid, several 25-watt solar panels and a wind turbine may be enough to help them get the power they need throughout the day. This method works best if you live further south, where there is a lot of sunlight. Solar power will help to power up your home without causing harm to the earth or having to rely on the local government to help keep the power going.

The wind turbine will be the backup in this situation on days when the sun does not shine. Think about the method you will use to store the power if you make extra, so you have it on cloudy and non-windy days.

Add a wood-burning stove: You will need a source of firewood. If you live in a wooded area, you can cut down dead trees for firewood. Start with a smaller model of a wood-burning stove to see how you like it and if you have a large enough supply of firewood.

Septic System and Waste Disposal

This is not the most fun part of living Off The Grid, but it is a fact of life. You will need to have a type of composting waste disposal system, or you can dig a more traditional septic system. Make sure to follow the federal and local guidelines for waste disposal. It is not just the law, but it is also sanitary.

You can also purchase self-contained composting toilets on Amazon.

Security Tips for Small Homes

Your small home will quickly become one of your most valuable possessions, along with the items you keep inside. This is the one place in the world where you want to feel safe and secure, and taking the right steps can make this a reality. Some of the tips you can use to keep your small home secure and safe include:

· Landscape with safety in mind: Take a walk around your property. Are there any places where a potential thief could hide and be hard to find? You do not need to cut down every tree and get rid of every bush, but if there is an area that is particularly overgrown, it may be a good idea to clean it up.

· Talk to the police department. Ask them about the neighborhood's safety or if they have some tips to help keep the area safe. A good website to check crime in any zip code in the US is https://spotcrime.com/

· Meet your neighbors. It is a good idea to become familiar with your neighbors. This is a great way to keep your property safe. When the neighbors know who you are, they are more likely to watch out for suspicious activity when you are away. When neighbors do not know each other, they may not notice when something goes wrong at your home.

· Pick the right lighting: Lighting can help set the right ambiance on the inside of the home. Outdoor lighting can help prevent your home from being targeted by thieves. While you do not want to blind the neighbors, going for motion-sensitive fixtures can provide light and security around the home.

· Avoid advertising when you shop: Porch pirating is becoming a big issue for many people. If you are planning to have a lot of packages delivered to your home, consider having them delivered to another location or require a signature before they are left. Be careful with the items you throw away. Thieves can look through the trash for signs of a new television or computer in the home.

· Set your safety routine: always establish a routine where you shut the windows, regularly lock the doors, and turn on the alarm system when it is time to leave your home. Never leave a spare key outside your door. Thieves know that homeowners do this and will know where to find it.

· Manage your visibility: Consider setting up methods to see who is at the front door before opening it. Do not place your valuables where they are seen from the street and do not place the home alarm panel in a place where people can see you arming it from the outside.

- A doorbell that has a camera or security lights with cameras can be very helpful if you are trying to see who is at your door or outside on your property.

· Protect the outdoor valuables: This will include your garages, sheds, and other outdoor buildings. Make sure you lock these nightly and secure anything that is left outside.

· Plan when away: There are times when you will need to be away from home. Do not make it obvious that you are not at home. Have your mail held, stop any papers to the home, and ask someone to stop by and check the home and remove any flyers. If you plan to be away for a long time, arrange for someone to handle the lawn mowing and snow removal too.

With a few precautions, your home can be a safe spot for you and your family to spend time.

How to Take Advantage of Outdoor Space

Many homeowners who choose to move into a small home will do so in a space that provides them with more land and space to be outside. Utilizing the space around your home, including the patio, can help make your small home seem less limiting, and it can get you closer to nature. Some ways that you can put your patio to use include:

Heat Things Up

Make your patio an extra room, even on those cold nights, by heating the area. Having a heat source available will help make the area more enjoyable and turn it into a nice social space for you and friends to gather. You can choose an outdoor heater, outdoor fireplace, or a cute firepit to provide warmth.

Add Lighting

When it comes to any area of your small home, lighting is important. And this is true of your patio area too. There are different lighting options that you can use. Lighting will be the most important when you get to the fall and winter months because it extends the amount of time you can spend on your patio. Set them up to a timer, so they automatically turn off when you are done. Options like spotlights, string lights, and path markers are good to use in this space. They sell bright solar motion lights and provide the extra light needed when walking to your front or back doors.

Weatherproof Furniture

Sitting on the patio, enjoying the fresh air, can be a great decision for those who live in a small home. You are more likely to use your patio if the area is comfortable and cozy. You need to consider weatherproof furniture to help make it durable, even when the weather goes south for you. Choose furniture made from the right materials like Sunbrella (fabric that resists sun fading) outdoor cushions so that they will last a long time and give you years of enjoyment.

Outdoor Kitchen

A small home means a small kitchen, so why not move some items outside. A grill or an outdoor kitchen can be a great decision to help give you more space. You can still have some of the kitchen appliances inside the home but moving the kitchen outside occasionally can be nice for enjoying the weather and entertaining guests for the holidays.

Outdoor Games are Fun

Add some games to the outdoor area to encourage the family to get outside and have some fun, no matter the weather. Yard games like ring toss or jump ropes are easy to store and a good place to start. You can also bring the TV out to a covered patio and watch the big game.

Conclusion

Bigger is not always better when it comes to the place you call home. There are so many people competing to have a bigger and better house than the next person. They can become house poor and have more home than they will ever really need. This can make them have to work all the time to pay the bills, and they miss out on all the things that are really important in life.

As we have explored in this beginner's guidebook, there is a better way.

It is easy to worry that a tiny home, or even a small home, will be too hard to turn into a place you can know and love. It does require a change in mindset and a hard look at what is valuable and what is taking up space in your life. But all the benefits can make it an adventure worth it for everyone in your family.

In this guidebook, we worked to prepare you for tiny home living. Just like purchasing a big, traditional home, many steps need to happen to make it a reality. From picking out a small home to downsizing and learning how to make more fit in less space. Moving into a small home is not something you do on a whim. With a little planning and preparation, and the many tips in this guidebook, you will be able to turn this into an exciting adventure that gives you the freedom, both financially and personally, that you only dreamed about.

Now that you have some tools and knowledge about living in a tiny or small home, go out there and start planning for small home living!

Check out my website for our other Books and Authors!

www.MediaHomeHarmony.com

Annette Maria Williams

- **Home Clutter Cleanse: An Essential Step-by-Step Guide to Organizing your House, Office and Life by Giving All Your Stuff a Home**

OUR OTHER AUTHORS-

Captain Jack

- Don't Rock the Boat: A Boating Logbook

Sally LaValley

- Dot Markers Activity Book for Kids: Learn Letters, Numbers and Shapes

- Handwriting Practice Workbook for Kids: Numbers, Letters-Activity and Tracing Book for Ages 3+

- Easter Dot Markers Activity Book for Kids: Learn Letter and Numbers

References

Adams, K. (2016, October 7). *How to Make a Room Look Less Crowded*. Home Guides | SF Gate. https://homeguides.sfgate.com/make-room-look-less-crowded-55051.html

In-text citation

Berry, K. (2021, July 27). *How to Organize Dining Rooms*. Housewife How-Tos. https://housewifehowtos.com/get-organized/organizing-the-dining-table/

Brennan, A., & Ebert, J. (2021, October 12). *Small living room lighting ideas – 25 well-lit ways to enhance a compact space*. Homesandgardens.Com. https://www.homesandgardens.com/spaces/decorating/small-living-room-lighting-ideas-223311

C., W. (2022, March 20). *Post author: William C*. Super Tiny Homes. https://www.supertinyhomes.com/tiny-houses-history/

Conaboy, K. (2015, July 28). *A Pint-Sized Nightmare: Five Couples Speak Out About Tiny Home Horrors*. Gawker. https://www.gawker.com/a-pint-sized-nightmare-five-couples-speak-out-about-ti-1720615844

Elliott, S. (2020, August 20). *10 Ways to Use Your Vertical Space*. HowStuffWorks. https://home.howstuffworks.com/home-decor/decorating-styles-techniques/10-ways-to-use-your-vertical-space.htm

Got a Moment? 20 Small-Space Decorating Mistakes to Avoid. (2021, May 19). MyDomaine. https://www.mydomaine.com/small-space-decorating-mistakes-4767886#:%7E:text=20%20Mistakes%20to%20Avoid%20When%20Decorating%20Small%20Spaces,Small%20Furniture%20in%20Excess.%20...%20More%20items...%20

Groner, R. (2021a, December 14). *5 Big Benefits of Living in a Small House | Perks of a Small Home.* Living Well Spending Less®. https://www.livingwellspendingless.com/5-big-benefits-living-small-house/amp/&ved=2ahUKEwi4-/

Groner, R. (2021b, December 14). *5 Big Benefits of Living in a Small House | Perks of a Small Home.* Living Well Spending Less®. https://www.livingwellspendingless.com/5-big-benefits-living-small-house/amp/

How to Organize a Dining Room. (2020). House Wife How Tos. https://housewifehowtos.com/get-organized/organizing-the-dining-table/

Ilijasic, T. T. (2022, March 4). *22 Tiny House Statistics, Fact, and Trends for 2022.* ComfyLiving. https://comfyliving.net/tiny-house-statistics/

L. (2020, August 18). *9 Important Tips on How to Choose Curtains.* Livspace Magazine. https://www.livspace.com/in/magazine/how-to-choose-curtains-and-drapes-for-your-windows/amp

Living in tiny homes was much harder than these people realized. (2016, September 27). Business Insider. https://www.businessinsider.com/five-people-who-abandoned-their-tiny-homes-2015-7?international=true&r=US&IR=T

Lyons, J. (2021, November 1). *How to Choose the Right Real Estate Agent.* Home Sellers Guide. https://www.zillow.com/sellers-guide/choose-right-real-estate-agent/amp/

NerdWallet. (2019). *How Much House Can I Afford? Affordability Calculator.* https://www.nerdwallet.com/mortgages/how-much-house-can-i-afford

Porter, I. (2019, August 19). *Future Planning & Your Home: What Decisions You Should Start Thinking About*. Ingrid Porter Interiors. https://ingridporter.com/future-planning-your-home-what-decisions-you-should-start-thinking-about/

press profile homify. (2022, February 18). *How To Choose The Right Flowers For Your Home*. Homify.Com. https://www.homify.com/ideabooks/7960937/how-to-choose-the-right-flowers-for-your-home

Rieland, B. R. (2018, April 26). *What Tiny Home Living Is Really Like*. AARP. https://www.aarp.org/home-family/your-home/info-2018/tiny-home-living-personal-stories.html

Sullivan, S. (2021). *Why Are Tiny Houses Built On Trailers & Wheels? (Explained)*. Www.Godownsize.Com. https://www.godownsize.com/why-tiny-houses-trailers-wheels/

T. (2021, March 2). *The Ultimate List Of Tiny Home Communities*. All About Tiny Houses. https://allabouttinyhouses.com/588/the-ultimate-list-of-tiny-home-communities/#:%7E:text=1%20Sustainability.%20TIny%20house%20villages%20are%20often%20built,are%20often%20more%20community%20activities%20you%20can%20join.

Turner, T. (2015, December 15). *Put your walls to work!* Yanko Design - Modern Industrial Design News. https://www.yankodesign.com/2015/12/15/put-your-walls-to-work/

White, M. (2018, January 29). *Where to Buy a Tiny House on Wheels*. Moving.Com. https://www.moving.com/tips/where-to-buy-a-tiny-house-on-wheels/

Yale, A. J. (2022, January 5). *13 Tips for First-Time Homebuyers: Your Must-Know Advice*. Credible. https://www.credible.com/blog/mortgages/first-time-homebuyer-tips/ https://upgradedhome.com/tiny-house-dimensions/